Read Music from Scratch

Neil Sissons

A co

PREFACE

Every week I receive hundreds of letters and emails from youngsters requesting pieces of classical music for inclusion in *The Classic FM School Run*, a feature that runs during my programme every morning just after eight o'clock. I never cease to be delighted by the passion and excitement that these young people feel for the music we play on Classic FM. Many of them want to hear professional musicians playing works that they themselves are learning at school. Others request favourite pieces, which they hope to be able to play in the future. Above everything, all of them have discovered the fun that can be had both from making and listening to music.

Henry Kelly
October 2001

Introduction

Read Music from Scratch is a complete guide to reading music which can be used by anybody who wants to understand more about what written music means. You don't have to play a musical instrument to use this book. Maybe you want to learn how to read song sheets, or to start writing your own music down. Or perhaps you go to concerts or listen to music and want to understand how it works on a page. The book will help you do all this, as well as making music-reading easier if you are learning an instrument for the first time.

How the book is organised
Learning to read music is just like learning any other language. There are various steps which are simple on their own, but which combine to give quite complicated results. This book is written so that you learn information a step at a time, and gradually combine them.

There are tags which contain reminders, hints and directions to other parts of the book. Try to keep an eye on these as you go through, as they will help you to remember new concepts and to navigate your way around the book.

On pages 78 and 79 there is a summary of all the words and ideas you have learned. If you need a reminder about something, look here first – it tells you where in the book it is explained.

Tags like this contain hints and tips

Getting started
The book begins with a guided tour of written music which shows you what many of the different signs and symbols actually do.

A few more hints
People learn at different speeds. It doesn't matter how quickly you work through the book. The important thing is to understand each page before you go on to the next one. But it's also important to go back through the book and revise things you already know. Sometimes you have to go back and look at a section you have done before, but in a different way.

Using the CD

The CD with this book will help you hear what signs and symbols mean when they are translated into sounds. Each new idea has examples on the CD so that you can read about it then hear the effect. The symbol in the margin (shown on the right) tells you which track to select.

Instructions in the text by the CD symbol tell you what to do. Sometimes you just have to listen. Others are games and exercises to help you go over what you have learned, and might ask you to clap, count or sing along. These exercises really will help you match up how music looks with how it sounds, and, importantly, how it feels.

03

A guided tour of written music

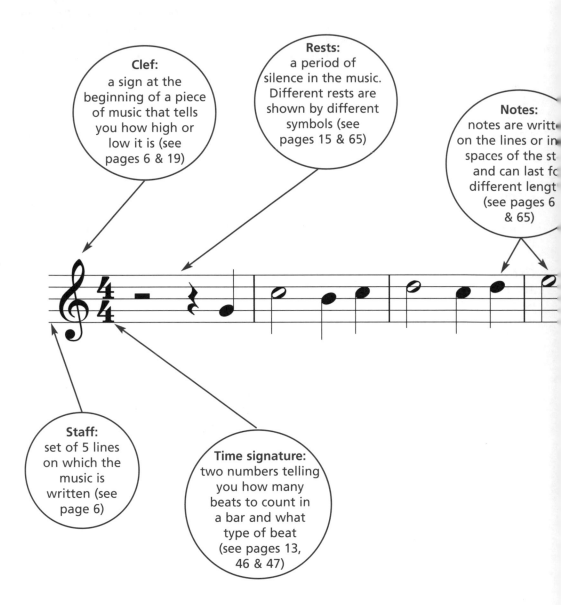

Clef:
a sign at the beginning of a piece of music that tells you how high or low it is (see pages 6 & 19)

Rests:
a period of silence in the music. Different rests are shown by different symbols (see pages 15 & 65)

Notes:
notes are writt. on the lines or in spaces of the st. and can last fc different lengt (see pages 6 & 65)

Staff:
set of 5 lines on which the music is written (see page 6)

Time signature:
two numbers telling you how many beats to count in a bar and what type of beat (see pages 13, 46 & 47)

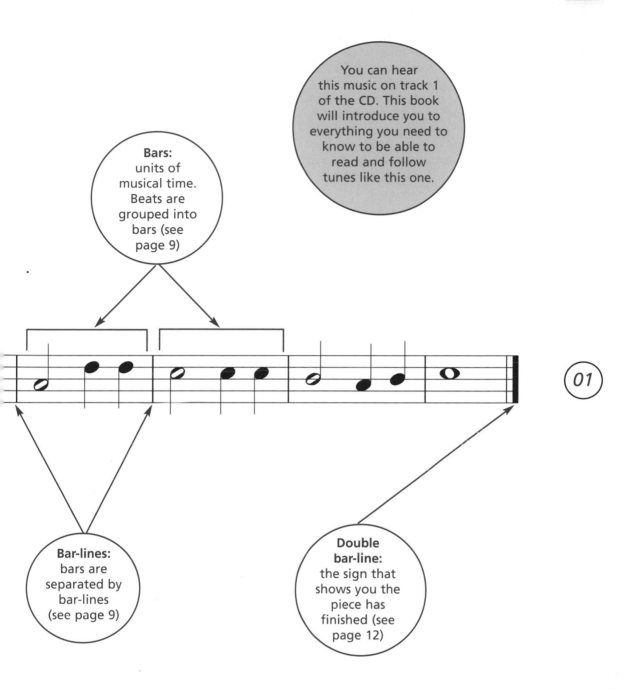

Bars: units of musical time. Beats are grouped into bars (see page 9)

You can hear this music on track 1 of the CD. This book will introduce you to everything you need to know to be able to read and follow tunes like this one.

Bar-lines: bars are separated by bar-lines (see page 9)

Double bar-line: the sign that shows you the piece has finished (see page 12)

01

High and low

 01 Play track 1 (or hum the beginning of *My Grandfather's Clock*) once more as you look at the line of blobs on the right. Can you run your finger from blob to blob as the music plays? Each blob shows a single sound in the tune. In music, these sounds are called notes, and the height or depth of a note is called its pitch. Pitch is one of the most important aspects of music, and learning about it is the first step to reading music.

Can you see how the blobs rise and fall as the notes in the tune rise and fall?

01 Did you see how the blobs move up and down as the notes rise and fall? To make the rising and falling blobs easier to read, we can link all the notes that are the same pitch – the same height or depth – by putting a line through them. Listen to track 1 again and look at the blobs to the right.

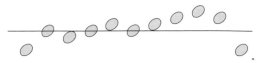

All blobs on the same line play the same note

In written music, notes are usually placed on a set of five lines called a staff, which makes them even easier to read. Notes are written either on the lines or in the spaces between them. Listen to track 1 one last time, and follow the music.

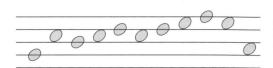

All blobs on the same line or space play the same note

How high? How low?

02 Now listen to track 2 of the CD. You will hear two versions of the row of notes shown above. Play it a few times, and follow the music as you watch the notes. The music fits with both versions, but the two versions are different. In what way?

The difference is that the first version is higher than the second. Each one begins on a different pitch. So the note-heads show you the rise and fall of the tune, but they don't show you how high or low it is. You need more information for this.

Fixing the pitch

03 Pitch is described using the first seven letters of the alphabet - A, B, C, D, E, F and G. All pitches can be described using these letter names. Notes on a stave need to be given a specific pitch. This is done using a clef, which indicates which pitch goes on each line or space.

In science, pitch is measured in units called hertz (after the physicist Heinrich Hertz). Any pitch can be measured in hertz (hz). The pitch on track 3 of the CD is 440 hz and is called A. In music it is written on the second space up in the staff. This is the note that orchestras always tune to.

The most common clef is the treble clef, which is sometimes called the G clef because it starts on the line that represents G.

The note A on different instruments

Here is where you will find the note A on several different instruments.

by plucking the second string from the right on a violin

by covering the back hole and top two front holes on a recorder

A

by finding the group of three black notes nearest the middle of a piano or keyboard and pressing the white key between the upper two black ones

Other notes and their names

Pitch names go in alphabetical order from A to G, then start again at A once more. Below you can see a set of pitches in the treble clef and their names. Now listen to the pitches shown (CD track 4) as they are played slowly. Try to sing along with the recording, singing the name of each note as it plays. Try it on your own too. It is good to practise singing the major scale, as this pattern of notes is called, because so much music is based on it, and if you have the scale in your head, it makes reading music much easier.

C   D   E   F   G   A   B   C   04

Now look at the pitches shown in the music below. Based on what you heard in the example above, can you imagine what the music below will sound like?

When you have tried to imagine the sound of the notes below, and to hum or sing them, listen to track 5 of the CD. How close were you?

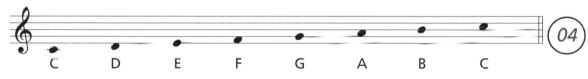

05

Using your imagination

A lot of reading music is about imagining in your head what music will sound like. Try reading the three sets of pitches below and try to hum or sing them to yourself.

When you have tried this, listen to the three sets of pitches on track 6 of the CD to see how close you were. Keep coming back to this exercise, as repeating it will help you to imagine notes more easily.

06

Long and short

If you tried to read the music against the CD on pages 4 and 5, you might still have found it hard to follow using just the blobs, because some of the notes last longer than others. As well as high and low, music is made up of patterns of long and short. These patterns are called rhythm. Listen to track 1 of the CD again. Listen for long and short this time, running your finger from box to box.

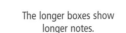

The longer boxes show longer notes.

The shorter boxes show shorter notes

Long, short, high, low

Written music is convenient because each note tells you both how high or low it is and how long or short it is. It's as if you had the boxes above combined with the pitches on the staff. Listen to track 1 again, whilst looking at the staff opposite.

Measuring long and short

Now we need to look at how you measure long and short sounds in music, and how they are written down. You measure the length of sounds against a steady pulse called a beat. The beat is regular, like a clock ticking. Listen to the beat on track 7 of the CD. There is exactly the same amount of time between each click. If you made a diagram of this, it might look something like the one on the right – a series of regular marks.

In music, the steady pulse is called a beat . . .

. . . and any individual click in that pulse is also called a beat

■ ■ ■ ■ ■ ■ ■ ■ ■ ■ ■

The beat is always regular but the rhythm may not be.

Try clapping or tapping a pencil along with track 7 until you feel familiar with it. Once you can do this, try singing the opening of *My Grandfather's Clock* over the top. (If you find this hard, listen to track 1 again to remind yourself how it goes.) If you had to draw a diagram of the rhythm of the start of the song, what would it look like in relation to the beat?

Beat or pulse ■ ■ ■ ■ ■ ■ ■ ■ ■ ■ ■ ■

Rhythm ■ ■ ■ ■ ■ ■ ■ ■ ■

Each long note lasts for two beats.

But the two short notes last for just one beat.

Now try counting – starting at 1 – along with the pulse on track 7. Can you keep counting until the clicks stop? How far did you get? The trouble with counting like this is that it isn't much help. For example, if written music told you to play a particular note on the 185th beat, you would have difficulty keeping count. Instead, beats are grouped into small units called bars.

1 2 3 4 5 6 7 8 9 10

■ ■ ■ ■ ■ ■ ■ ■ ■ ■

Bars and beats

Almost all music is divided up into groups of beats called bars. You can have any number of beats in a bar, but it is rare to have more than twelve. The most common number of beats in a bar is four. Bars are separated from each other by a vertical line called a barline. In the diagram opposite, there is a barline after every fourth beat. This tells you to start counting again at "1" after every barline.

1   2   3   4 | 1   2   3   4 | 1   2   3   4 |

Counting bars

Music is not only divided into bars because it is easier than having one long string of notes. It is also because most music falls naturally into groups of beats. If you say the words of *My Grandfather's Clock* out loud, you can hear this. You feel as though you want to emphasise some parts of some words, making them louder or 'heavier' than others. If you were to write the louder bits in heavier type than the others, you would probably get the effect below:

My **Grand**father's clock was too **tall** for the shelf, so it **stood** ninety years on the **floor**. It was **tall**er by far than the **old** man himself, though it **weighed** not a pennyweight **more**.

Now play the pulse on track 7 again and say the words above over the top a few times. How many beats are there between each word in heavy type? If you count each heavy-type word as 'one', what number have you counted to before you get to the next?

The answer is that you have to count to four before between one heavy-type word and the next. This means that *My Grandfather's Clock* has four beats in each bar. You can show this in a diagram, putting the beats over words and a barline after every fourth beat.

07

|1   2   3   4 |1   2   3   4 |
My **Grand**father's clock was too **tall** for the shelf, so it
    1   2   3   4 |1 2 3 4 |
    stood ninety years on the **floor**.   It was
    1 2   3   4 |1   2   3   4 |
    taller by far than the **old** man himself, though it
    1   2   3   4 |1   2 3 4 |
    weighed not a pennyweight **more**.   It was bought . . .

Writing rhythms down

In music, one-beat notes are shown like the ones in the diagram below. Barlines are used to break up the notes into bars.

Try counting the pulse while clapping the one-beat notes:

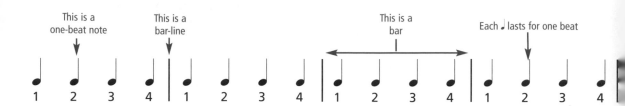

This is a one-beat note

This is a bar-line

This is a bar

Each ♩ lasts for one beat

1 2 3 4 | 1 2 3 4 | 1 2 3 4 | 1 2 3 4

Combining pitch and rhythm

When notes are written on the staff, they combine information about pitch with information about rhythm. The rhythmic information is shown in various ways. For example, look at the one-beat notes above. To write a one-beat note you need two different parts – the notehead and the stem. Between them, the notehead and the stem contain a lot of information.

The colour of the notehead is important. If you give the one-beat note above a hollow notehead instead of a filled one, you make a note that lasts for two beats (in general, filled noteheads show notes with shorter time values, while hollow noteheads show notes with longer time values). And the stem is important too. A note with a hollow head without a stem lasts for four beats.

Lines and spaces

The pitch of the note is shown by the position of the notehead on the staff, as shown on page 7, and also by a clef such as the treble clef (shown on page 6). Every staff has 11 different "slots" for notes – six spaces and five lines. And there are other ways of increasing the number of notes on the staff – you can read about these later on in the book.

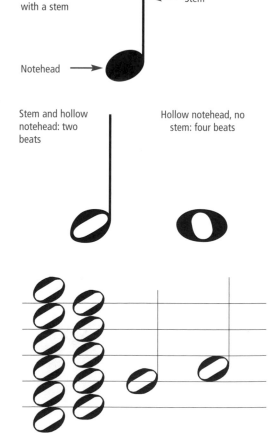

One-beat note: filled-in notehead with a stem

Stem

Notehead

Stem and hollow notehead: two beats

Hollow notehead, no stem: four beats

Starting to read pitch and rhythm together

When notes are written on the staff, a note which lasts for one beat (a single click on track 7) is written like this and is called a crotchet or quarter note.

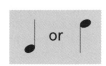

A note which lasts for two beats (two clicks on track 7) is written like this and is called a minim or half note.

A note which lasts for four beats (four clicks on track 7) is written like this and is called a semibreve or whole note.

Now listen to track 8 as you look at the music. Watch how the notation shows both the length of the notes and the shape of the melody as it rises and falls. Every note shows how long it is and how high or low it is.

Try reading for yourself

Now look at the music below, which is a well-known tune. Before you play it on track 9 of the CD, can you recognise it from the way the notes rise and fall? Or perhaps from the rhythm (try tapping it over the beat on track 7, watching closely for the two-beat notes). Once you have tried imagining what the music sounds like, can you name the tune? Now play track 9 to see whether you were right.

This is all that reading music is – looking at pitches and rhythms and imagining (or playing) the sounds they make. This is what singers and instrumentalists are doing when they read music. Although they are turning that imagined sound into sound you can hear, first of all they are 'thinking the music'. No matter what you want to do with music, you have to be able to 'think' it first.

Rhythm versus beat

We have already seen how notes are grouped together in bars to help you follow the rhythm of a melody. This also helps you to keep your place when the melody is long.

In the music below, the melody has been divided into groups of four beats, exactly as we did at the bottom of page 9. To help you count while you are learning, the beats are shown under the music,

numbered 1, 2, 3, 4. Each minim or half note has two counts under it, while each crotchet or quarter note has just one.

This gives you the same type of information as the diagram at the top of page 8, but in a more efficient way. In written music, you know how long a note is as soon as you see it because you know how many beats it lasts for – you don't have to measure how much space it takes up.

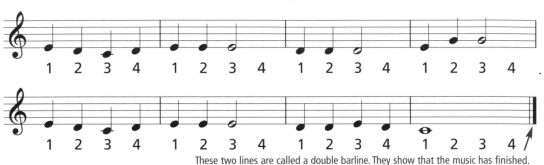

These two lines are called a double barline. They show that the music has finished.

The beat doesn't stop

In most music, the beat carries on whatever happens. In a long piece, it may change, or it may speed up or slow down, but it hardly ever stops until the music finishes. Listen to track 10. Before the music starts, you will hear four clicks

which mark the beat. Try to follow the music above, by counting 1, 2, 3, 4 along with the clicks. You will see that though the tune contains notes of different lengths, the beat keeps going without changing.

Adding in barlines

Below is the music that you tried to read on the previous page, but the barlines have been missed out. Can you draw them in after every four beats?

Remember that minims or half notes count for 2 beats each. It might help to

listen to track 9 again to hear the pattern of long and short notes. (If you want to check your answer, look at the music on the previous page.)

When you have done this, try clapping and counting the result to check it works.

Different music, different beat

Now listen to the music on track 11 of the CD. It is a tune called *Barcarolle* by the composer Offenbach, who lived in the 19th century. Can you count the beat along with it? Can you clap every first beat? Can you feel a regular four-beat pulse?

It is unlikely that you managed to do this. Even if you could feel the pulse and clap every first beat, you will not have been able to count in groups of four. Why? Look at *Barcarolle* written down. Does the music give you any clues? How many beats are there between each barline?

(11)

The answer is that in *Barcarolle* the beat is in groups of three, not four. This is what makes it feel different from track 9. Listen again while you look at the music, and count the beats out loud. Then play the track once more. This time, see whether you can tap with your left hand on beat 1 and your right hand on beats 2 and 3. This should help you to feel the three beat pattern. You should also have noticed a new length of note - a minim (two-beat note) with a dot after it. This lasts for three beats. There is more about dotted notes on page 26.

Beats in a bar

Now look at the two examples below: one shows the opening of *Twinkle Twinkle*, and the other the opening of *Barcarolle*. To the right of the clef you will see two numbers, one above the other. These numbers are called the time signature and they tell you how many beats you have to count in each bar.

How time signatures work

A time signature is made up of two numbers. The number on the top tells you how many beats there are in each bar. The number on the bottom tells you what kind of beats they are. 4/4 tells you that there are 4 ♩ beats in each bar, 3/4 means that there are 3 ♩ beats in each bar and 2/4 means that there are 2 ♩ beats in each bar. You can find out about other time signatures later on in the book.

The top number tells you there are four beats in each bar.

The 4 on the bottom means the beats are crotchets or quarter notes

More about time signatures

All the melodies you have heard so far have been in 4/4 except for *Barcarolle*. Now listen to the tunes on tracks 12, 13 and 14 of the CD. Can you tell whether they are in 3/4 time or 4/4 time?

Look at the music below. Each line shows the opening of one of the tunes you have just heard, but not in the same order. Which one is which? Write the track number in the circle provided.

Now, for each tune:

1 sing the opening from the music

2 add in the missing time signatures and barlines

You can check your answers on page 75. If you need help, listen to the CD a few times.

More about beats and bars

Now look at the music below as you listen to track 15. It is in 4/4 time, so we know that there are four beats in each bar. But how many beats are there in the first bar? You probably noticed that there are three notes in the first bar instead of four.

Tunes do not have to begin on the first beat of the bar. Some tunes have one note before the first strong beat: look at 'My **Grand**father's clock' on page 9. Other tunes may have two or three notes before the first strong beat.

Not all tunes begin on the first beat of the bar.

You will probably have noticed some other symbols in this music that we have not yet met; these are rests.

Sounds and silence

Listen to track 16. Can you hear that the melody includes moments of silence? Listen again and tap the beat. Keep on tapping through the whole tune, and listen out for the one-beat notes, the two-beat notes and the silences. How many beats do the silences last for?

Reading rests in written music
Listen to track 16 again, tapping two beats for the two-beat rests and one beat for the one-beat rest. Look at the music below as you listen. Can you see where the rests come? Count these just like you would notes.

Silences in music are called rests. They are shown by special symbols.

This rest lasts for one beat. It is called a crotchet rest or quarter rest.

For two-beat rests, you either see two crotchet rests or a minim rest like this.

At first, try saying "rest" aloud for each beat of rest

The instruments of the orchestra

By the Classical period (the time of Mozart and Haydn), orchestras would typically contain two each of flutes, oboes, clarinets and bassoons, as well as two horns, two trumpets, two timpani and strings.

Later, more instruments were added. The list on the opposite page is arranged in the order that the parts would appear in a score. This represents the usual Romantic orchestra, though other instruments (such as the contra bassoon or the alto flute) might also be added. Sometimes there are three of each wind instrument and there would usually be four horns, three trombones and a tuba. One or two harps were often included.

The orchestra for a modern piece might additionally include saxophone(s), extra percussion (such as xylophone, marimba, gongs and drumkit) as well as at least three timpani. Piano is often included too.

The music of an orchestral piece is known as the score

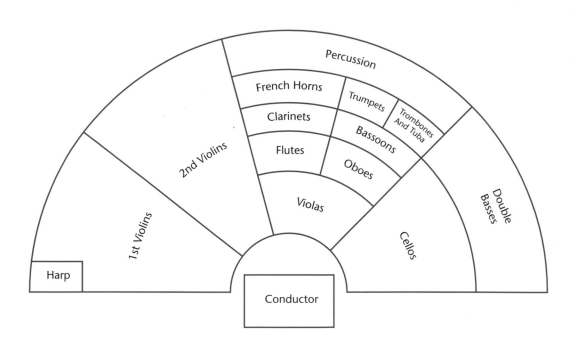

Percussion

French Horns

Trumpets

Trombones And Tuba

Clarinets

Bassoons

2nd Violins

Flutes

Oboes

Double Basses

Violas

1st Violins

Cellos

Harp

Conductor

The sections of the orchestra

The woodwind, brass and string sections each consist of groups of instruments which cover the whole range of notes, from low bass to very high treble sounds. This means that each section can play alone, or be blended with others. Also, pairs of different instruments can play the same thing together to give a fuller or more interesting sound.

when instruments play the same notes together it is know as doubling

THE WOODWIND

The wind section consists of (from the highest to the lowest) *piccolos, flutes, oboes, clarinets and bassoons*.

The *piccolo* is really just a small *flute*, and plays an octave higher. Its piercing high notes can cut through the sound of the whole orchestra (as in the storm music in Beethoven's *Pastoral Symphony*). *Oboes* have a more buzzing tone than the smooth sounding *clarinet*, and sometimes the *cor anglais* (which is a larger oboe) is added. This is the instrument which plays the famous melody in the slow movement of Dvořàk's *New World Symphony*. The bass notes are provided by the *bassoons*.

THE BRASS

The bright sound of the *trumpets* provide the highest notes, with the very versatile *french horns* providing the middle range sounds.

There are usually alto and tenor *trombones*, so that they can provide bass notes as well as middle ones. The trombones are used in loud, full orchestral passages because of their powerful sound.

The *tuba* plays the bass notes, though it can play surprisingly high, if necessary.

THE PERCUSSION

The percussion is divided into tuned and untuned sections.

The untuned instruments (various *drums*, *cymbals*, etc.) do not play specific notes, but add to the musical atmosphere.

The tuned section includes instruments such the *glockenspiel*, the *vibraphone* and the *tubular bells*, all of which can play melodically. The *timpani* can be tuned to a limited number of notes (which the composer chooses) which are used to dramatically reinforce the bass line.

THE STRINGS

The string instruments are very similar in appearance and sound, and just differ in pitch.

The *violins* are the highest and are split into two groups (first and second violins). The *violas* play mid-range notes and the *cellos* the bass notes (although they can also play higher melodies very effectively, when a rich sound is required). The *double basses* very often play the same notes as the cellos but an octave lower, though in the third movement of Beethoven's *Fifth Symphony* they have a very fast solo passage.

New notes

Now look at the music below. As you can see, some extra notes have been added (marked D E F and G). They continue the scale upwards, each with its own line or space.

D   E   F   G

17 Listen to track 17, which plays this new, longer version of the C major scale you first saw on page 7. Listen carefully to the last 5 notes, then play the track again to hear the first five. Can you hear how the last five notes are higher versions of the first five?

In music, the distance from any note to the one of the same name above or below it is called an octave. The gap between the two C notes in the music above, or the two Ds, is an octave. Can you draw lines on the music below to link the notes that are an octave apart?

18 Below is the music to a famous tune which uses some of these extra notes. Listen to it on track 18 as you follow the music. Can you spot the notes which are higher or lower versions of each other? (The correct notes are shown on page 75.)

19 As you have heard, these new notes are the same as the lower notes C, D, E, F and G, but one octave higher. We can also use these notes to write some of the earlier tunes in this book an octave higher. Look at the music below. Do you recognise it? Try to read it, then listen to track 19 to hear if you imagined it correctly.

Higher and higher

Now look at *Baa Baa Black Sheep* below. As this tune goes higher than G, we need to write notes that are higher than the top of the staff. As you can see, the notes above G are arranged so that they each go on (or between) small extra lines which extend the staff. These are called leger lines. Listen to track 20 and follow the notes in the music as you go.

This note is A. It sits on one leger line above the treble staff

B sits on top of one leger line above the treble staff

C sits on two leger lines above the treble staff

The leger lines can extend the range of notes far beyond this C; flute music, for example, regularly uses notes with as many as 5 leger lines.

. . . and lower and lower

You can also use leger lines below the treble staff too, in exactly the same way. In fact, the C you have already learned which sits below the treble staff has a leger line of its own. To go below this note, you just add more leger lines and work downwards.

This note is G below middle C – the lowest note on a violin

But what happens if you need to write much lower notes? Most of the notes on a bassoon, a cello or a trombone, for example, are a lot lower than this C, and it isn't easy to read lots of leger lines. For these notes, you need a different clef, called the bass clef.

The bass clef

Below is the scale of C major, an octave lower than the version on page 7. Listen to this on track 21 while you look at the music.

Reading the bass clef

The bass clef curls round the second line down on the staff. The two dots sit either side of this line. They tell you that the note on the line between the dots is F.

Now you know this note, can you write the names of the other notes underneath this scale? (The answer is on page 75.)

F

Listen to track 21 again, and look at the music above. Then play track 4 and look at the music below. Can you hear how the C scale in the bass clef is just the same, but

lower than the treble version?
Try writing the names of the treble clef notes underneath the music. (See page 75 for the answer.)

You may have noticed that the notes in the bass clef are not in the same places as in the treble clef. For example, in the bass clef low C is in the second space up, while the note in the second space up in the treble clef is A.

From low to high

Now look at the music below and listen to track 22. You can follow the C major scale down and back up again. Can you see how the notes in the bass clef follow downwards from the notes in the treble

clef? The bass clef is used for lower instruments such as bassoon or cello. It is also used for the lower notes in keyboard music (those that are usually played with the left hand).

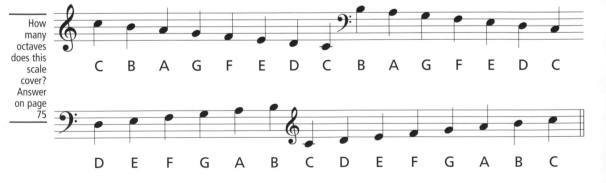

How many octaves does this scale cover? Answer on page 75

C B A G F E D C B A G F E D C

D E F G A B C D E F G A B C

Moving between treble and bass clefs

Sometimes it is useful to write a tune in more than one clef, moving between treble and bass as necessary.

Look at the music below. Can you read the tune? Try following the hints opposite and see if you can imagine how the music sounds. This isn't easy, but after a bit of practice you will get the hang of it. Again, this is a famous tune – can you tell what it is?

- What note does the music start on? Try naming all the notes.

- How many beats are there in each bar? Try counting and clapping the rhythm.

- Now try singing the tune. If you have difficulty finding any of the notes, listen to them again on track 22.

Once you have tried this, listen to track 23. Did you guess the tune correctly?

Two clefs, two lines of music

Having two clefs is also useful because you can use them together to show two lines of music at the same time. Look at the music below.

In the treble clef is the melody of the folk song *Early One Morning*. In the bass clef there is a bass line which fits with it.

Listen to track 24 and follow the treble clef part. Then listen to track 25 and follow the bass line. Can you see how the bass moves by step (on to the next note up or down)? Listen to each part a few times, until you are familiar with both of

them. When you are ready, listen to track 26 and try to follow both parts at once. To help you with this, the two parts are played on different instruments, the melody on an oboe and the bass line on a cello.

Shorter notes

27 Now listen to the tune on track 27 of the CD – an old English song called *Lavender's Blue*. Can you tell what the time signature should be? Listen again, tapping along to the beat. Listen out for the shorter notes: did you notice some notes were played more quickly than the beat?

Lavender's Blue is written down below. Can you spot the new shorter notes every time they appear? Clap the beat (which is three beats to the bar) as you listen again. How many of the shorter notes are there to each beat?

Half-beat notes

The answer is that there are two shorter notes for each beat. Each of these shorter notes occupies half a beat. Half-beat notes are called quavers or eighth notes. A half-beat note on its own has a curved tail. Half-beat notes are often joined together in groups of two or four by a line called a beam. When counting half-beat notes, it can help to say "one-and-two-and-three-and-four-and".

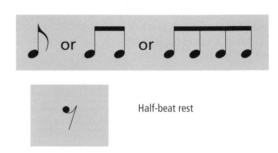

Half-beat rest

Look at the music below. This tune contains half-beat notes, and is divided between the two staves. In the fourth bar there is a half-beat rest, showing that there is half a beat of silence after the half-beat note in that bar. Listen to this tune on track 28, and follow the melody line in the music. Listen and look out for the half-beat rest.

Putting it all together ❶

Now it is time to look again at some of the things you have learned so far. Work slowly through this page and you will find that everything fits together easily. Start by looking at the music below. The idea is to try to imagine how the written music sounds before you listen to it on the CD. At the foot of this page you will find a list of where the things you need to know are explained, so if you are having difficulty, just follow the reminders.

Listen to track 29 to hear the 3/4 beat. Try to imagine the rhythm of the music above. Look at it carefully. How do you think the three bars with quaver rests will sound? Can you tap the rhythm along with the beat?

Now listen to track 30. You will hear the rhythm of the tune over the top of the beat. Listen a few more times, until you are familiar with it.

Writing what you hear
Now listen to track 31 again. Can you write the opening of the tune on the empty staff below? Doing this will help you to remember what you have learned.

Now look at the music above again. Can you tell what the melody sounds like? (If you want a hint, listen to the first few seconds of track 31 then stop the CD.) Look at the contours of the music. Where does it rise and fall? Try to match the pitches and the rhythm until you have a picture of the melody. Do you recognise it? When you have tried this listen to track 31 in full, following the shape of the melody carefully as you listen.

(Don't cheat – cover the music at the top of the page before you start!) Stop the CD if necessary to give yourself time to write. Don't forget the clef, time signature, rests . . .

29

30

31

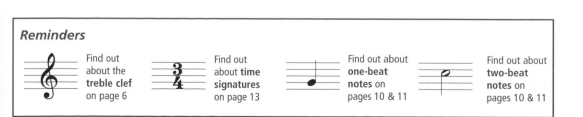

Reminders

| | Find out about the **treble clef** on page 6 | | Find out about **time signatures** on page 13 | | Find out about **one-beat notes** on pages 10 & 11 | | Find out about **two-beat notes** on pages 10 & 11 |

Putting it all together ❷

Try to imagine the rhythm of the music below, just as you did on the previous page. When you have thought it through a few times, try tapping it to the beat on track 29.

29

32 Check your rhythm by listening to track 32. Which parts of it are the same as the music on the previous page?

33 Look at the music above once more. This time, try to imagine what the notes will sound like. (If you want a hint about where to start, listen to the first few seconds of track 33.) Look at the contours of the music. Where does it rise and fall? Try to match the pitches and the rhythm until you have a picture of the music in your mind. When you have tried this listen to track 33 to hear it in full. Follow the shape of it as you listen.

Two parts together
When you know both these examples well, look at the music opposite. It combines both the previous examples in a two-part piece. You can hear this on track 34. When you listen to it at first, try following just one part at a time. Then listen again and try to follow both lines at once.

You can see examples of these rhythms on page 48

Quarter-beat notes

A quarter-beat note on its own has two curved tails. Quarter-beat notes are often joined together in groups of two or four by two lines called beams.

A quarter-beat note is called a semiquaver or sixteenth note. Four of them last one beat.

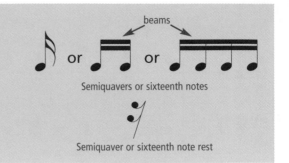

Semiquavers or sixteenth notes

Semiquaver or sixteenth note rest

A new rhythm

35
36

Listen and compare tracks 35 and 36, both versions of Chopin's *Funeral March*. Then try following the music while listening to these tracks.

The first version uses one-beat notes (crotchets) and half-beat notes (quavers), whereas the second replaces the pairs of quavers with the pattern

Here, the first quaver (eighth note) has been dotted and lasts three quarters of a beat. It is followed by a quarter-beat note (semiquaver). It is better to "feel" this kind of dotted rhythm than try to count it.

Listen a few times, until the dotted notes feel natural and you can tell the difference between the quavers which are dotted and the ones that are "straight".

Dotted rhythms explained

A dot to the right of a note tells you to increase its length by half as much again.

So a dot after a two-beat note means that you hold it for three beats rather than two. In 3/4 time, a three-beat note lasts for an entire bar.

A dot written after a crotchet or quarter note tells you to hold the note for one and a half beats.

A dotted quaver (or dotted eighth note) needs to be followed by a quarter-beat note to make a complete beat.

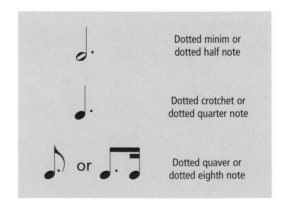

Dotted minim or dotted half note

Dotted crotchet or dotted quarter note

Dotted quaver or dotted eighth note

Try counting and then clapping the following rhythm.

37

Then listen to track 37 to hear if you were right.

Musical sentences

Listen and compare tracks 38 and 39, which are both versions of the tune *Early One Morning*. What is the difference between the two tracks?

Did you notice that the notes are played smoothly in groups on track 39? This helps you to hear the shape of the music. It is like listening to spoken words, with the gaps between the groups of notes being the full stops between the sentences.

Listen to track 39 again, this time following the music. The notes in each group are joined by a curved line: these lines are called phrase-marks, and the groups of notes are called phrases.

These marks are very important, as phrasing allows the music to sound natural and "breathe". It's the difference between saying a lot of words without pausing, and forming them into sentences or phrases.

Can you add phrase-marks to this tune? To help, listen to an unphrased version of it on track 31.

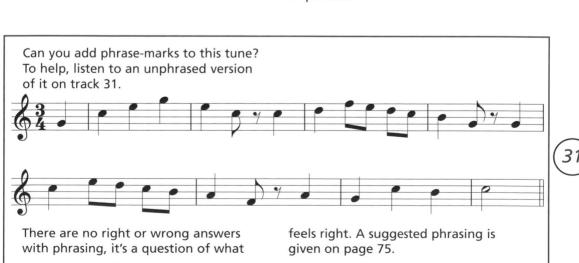

There are no right or wrong answers with phrasing, it's a question of what feels right. A suggested phrasing is given on page 75.

Musical punctuation

Just as written language has punctuation, written musical language has signs and symbols to make musical sense of phrases.

This is a more detailed form of punctuation than phrasing: a bit like the commas within sentences.

Slurs and legato

Bars are always counted from the first complete bar

The next piece, *Hunting Song*, uses a sign called a slur. This short curved line (which looks like a short phrase mark) tells you that the notes it connects have to be played smoothly, with no gaps between. Playing smoothly is called playing legato.

Staccato notes

Look at bar 4 of *Hunting Song*: there is a small dot placed above the third note in the bar (E). A dot like this above or below a note tells you that the note is very short – it stops almost as soon as you've heard it. This is known as staccato.

Signs telling you how loud or quiet to play or sing are called dynamics

Listen to *Hunting Song* on track 40. The staccato notes and slurs add character and feeling to the phrases. This process of giving the music shape by having some notes played smoothly and shortening others (or just leaving them as they are) is called articulation. Another type of articulation is an accent. This sign above or below a note means it should be played with an accent:

     or

Not all written music shows all the articulation needed to perform it. Many earlier composers, such as J.S. Bach, often left the performer to decide on their own articulation.

Dynamics

Dynamics are signs which indicate how loudly music is played. In this song, the phrases are shown by the dynamics: the *f* means loud and the *p* means soft. Other commonly used dynamics are:

mp means moderately quiet
mf means moderately loud
ff means very loud
pp means very quiet
crescendo or
      means gradually louder
diminuendo or
      means gradually softer

Tones and semitones

Look at the keyboard diagram on the right. The distance from any key to the one next to it on the right or left (black or white) is called a semitone.

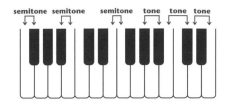

Most of the time a semitone is from a white key to a black key (or a black key to a white key) but on the keyboard there are some semitones from a white key to a white key. Can you see where?

The distance between any two notes is called an interval

The gap from any key to the one two steps away (black or white) is called a tone. Some examples of tones and semitones are shown in the diagram on the right.

Any major scale, like C major below, is a chain of tones and semitones. Going upwards, every one-octave major scale has tones and semitones in the following order:

TONE	TONE	SEMITONE	TONE	TONE	TONE	SEMITONE

The C major scale

In any major scale, most of the notes are a tone apart, in other words, there is a note between them which is not played. Some of the notes are only a semitone apart though. These semitone gaps have been marked with brackets.

Listen to track 4 and try to hear the difference between tones and semitones.

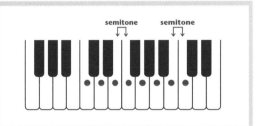

The semitones in the C major scale come between white notes which have no black note between them.

Some new notes

Listen again to track 4, following the music alongside. Keep looking at this music while you listen to track 41. Can you tell what is different?

There are more notes in the scale on track 41, twelve instead of seven (not counting the C at the top), but it still ends on the same note as the one in the written music. Some notes have been added which come in between the notes of the C major scale.

The chromatic scale

The scale with the extra notes is known as a chromatic scale, and uses all the notes of the keyboard, black as well as white. Follow the notes shown on this keyboard as you listen to track 41. All these notes are a semitone apart.

Accidentals

If we want to use one of the other notes, which is not in the scale of C, we can use "sharp" or "flat" signs. These symbols, which alter the pitch of a note, are known as accidentals.

Sharps

If you see a sharp sign in front of a note, it moves the note a semitone above the note that is written. Go one note higher up the chromatic scale.

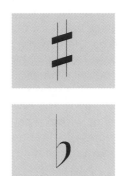

Flats

If you see a flat sign in front of a note, it moves the note a semitone below the written note. Go one note lower down the chromatic scale.

Naturals

This sign is called a natural. It is often used when a note with an accidental is followed in the same bar by the same note in its normal form. When this happens, a sign is needed to tell us that it is no longer a sharp or a flat.

Accidentals in scales

The music below is like a C major scale, but one note has been altered: the notes are played as normal, until you reach the F. Because of the sharp sign in front of it, the black note a semitone higher is played instead.

On track 42, listen carefully to how the fourth note (F) is now only a semitone away from the G. Compare the sound of this scale with the C major scale in which the F was closer to the note E (track 4).

The next scale is also like C major but with one note altered: again, the notes are played as normal, until you reach the E. Because of the flat sign in front of it, the black note a semitone lower is played instead.

Listen to this scale on track 43 to hear how the third note (E) is now only a semitone away from the D. Compare the sound of this new scale with the C major scale on track 4, in which the E was close to the note F.

Reading accidentals in music

Listen to *Greensleeves* on track 44, following the music below. The last note in bar 14 is marked with an asterisk. Did you spot that it was a sharp, like the first note in the bar? This is because an accidental sign doesn't just apply to the note it is next to. It lasts until the next bar-line. Every time the note appears in that bar, it is still a sharp or a flat.

Have a look at *Für Elise* by Beethoven. Notice how the first two times the note D appears, it is sharpened, but the third time, it has a ♮ sign in front of it. This shows that it goes back to being an ordinary D. Play track 45, listening carefully to the note D each time it appears. Can you hear the difference between the sharp and natural Ds?

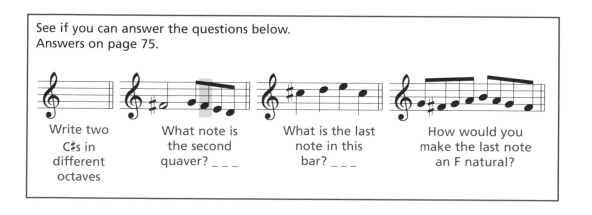

See if you can answer the questions below.
Answers on page 75.

Write two C♯s in different octaves

What note is the second quaver? _ _ _

What is the last note in this bar? _ _ _

How would you make the last note an F natural?

History of music at a glance

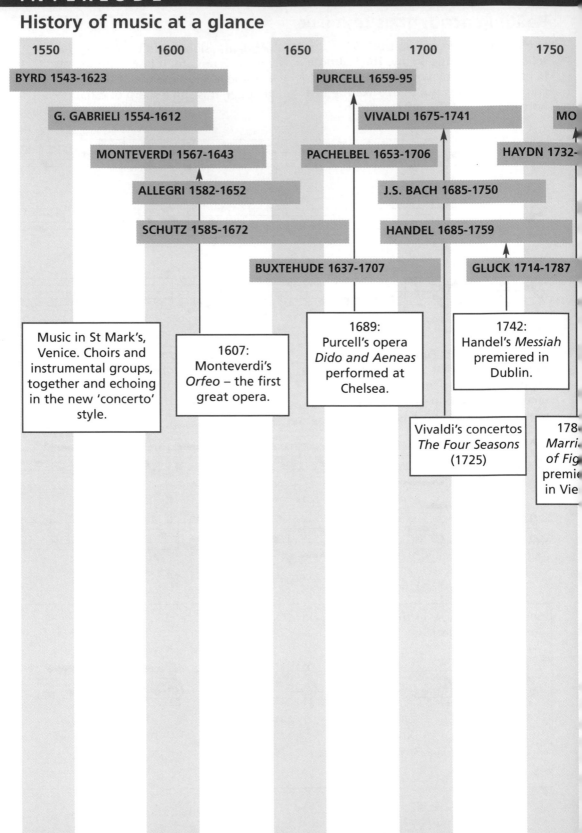

1550	1600	1650	1700	1750

BYRD 1543-1623

G. GABRIELI 1554-1612

MONTEVERDI 1567-1643

ALLEGRI 1582-1652

SCHUTZ 1585-1672

BUXTEHUDE 1637-1707

PURCELL 1659-95

VIVALDI 1675-1741

PACHELBEL 1653-1706

J.S. BACH 1685-1750

HANDEL 1685-1759

GLUCK 1714-1787

MO

HAYDN 1732-

Music in St Mark's, Venice. Choirs and instrumental groups, together and echoing in the new 'concerto' style.

1607: Monteverdi's *Orfeo* – the first great opera.

1689: Purcell's opera *Dido and Aeneas* performed at Chelsea.

1742: Handel's *Messiah* premiered in Dublin.

Vivaldi's concertos *The Four Seasons* (1725)

178
Marri
of Fig
premi
in Vie

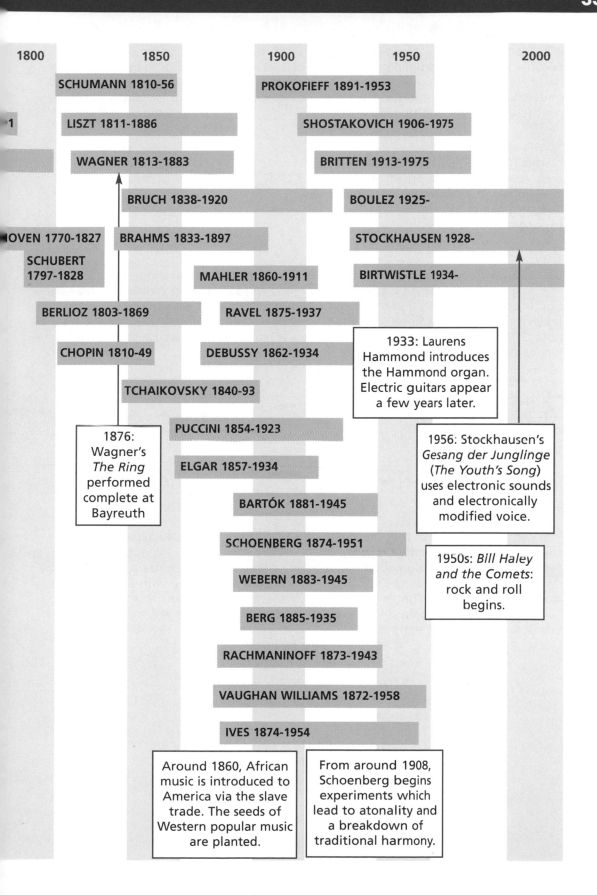

1800   1850   1900   1950   2000

SCHUMANN 1810-56

PROKOFIEFF 1891-1953

1

LISZT 1811-1886

SHOSTAKOVICH 1906-1975

WAGNER 1813-1883

BRITTEN 1913-1975

BRUCH 1838-1920

BOULEZ 1925-

OVEN 1770-1827   BRAHMS 1833-1897

STOCKHAUSEN 1928-

SCHUBERT
1797-1828

MAHLER 1860-1911

BIRTWISTLE 1934-

BERLIOZ 1803-1869

RAVEL 1875-1937

1933: Laurens
Hammond introduces
the Hammond organ.
Electric guitars appear
a few years later.

CHOPIN 1810-49

DEBUSSY 1862-1934

TCHAIKOVSKY 1840-93

PUCCINI 1854-1923

1876:
Wagner's
The Ring
performed
complete at
Bayreuth

ELGAR 1857-1934

1956: Stockhausen's
Gesang der Junglinge
(*The Youth's Song*)
uses electronic sounds
and electronically
modified voice.

BARTÓK 1881-1945

SCHOENBERG 1874-1951

1950s: *Bill Haley
and the Comets*:
rock and roll
begins.

WEBERN 1883-1945

BERG 1885-1935

RACHMANINOFF 1873-1943

VAUGHAN WILLIAMS 1872-1958

IVES 1874-1954

Around 1860, African
music is introduced to
America via the slave
trade. The seeds of
Western popular music
are planted.

From around 1908,
Schoenberg begins
experiments which
lead to atonality and
a breakdown of
traditional harmony.

Scales and keys

It is important to know about scales because they are the building blocks of music. Understanding scales will help you understand more about music. Over the next few pages you will find more information about scales and keys, and how they fit together to make music. To begin with, some of the most important words and ideas are explained here.

Scale

A scale is any series of notes that move by step. A scale can begin on any note and move upwards or downwards. Scales have different names, depending on what notes they contain.

Key

If a tune is based on the notes in the scale of C major, musicians say it is "in the key of C major". This means that the music feels complete when it finishes on the note C. It may begin on C as well. So far, nearly all the pieces in this book have been based around the scale of C major. Listen to *Lavender's Blue* on track 27 again and compare it with track 46. Can you hear the difference? The music on track 46 is higher. This is because the "home" note is not C but D.

You can see in this music that the shape of the melody remains exactly the same. In fact, each note in the original version is simply one note higher in the key of D. Now listen to track 47. That is how *Lavender's Blue* would sound in the home key of D without the F sharps.

In D major, the note F needs to be sharpened. If you look at the music you will see that the semitone intervals in the melody are marked with a bracket. The F sharp has to be there to make the melody sound the same as in C major.

Some new keys

Any melody can be moved to a different key. This is called transposing (or transposition). This is often done to make it easier to play or sing, but there is also a different "feel" to each key. There is a major key for each of the twelve notes in the "chromatic" scale (see page 29) and each one contains different sharp or flat notes. You can see all the different keys and scales on pages 72-73.

This might seem like a lot to remember, but the construction of a major scale is always the same (see page 29).

Starting to read music in different keys

Look at these two keyboards. In the first, you can see the notes of C major scale, which uses all the white notes.

If you start on the note D and move upwards using just the white notes you'll get a different pattern of tones and semitones. To get the correct pattern of tones and semitones you will need a scale with two sharps in it.

On the blank keyboard picture here, see if you can put in the notes for a scale of E major. Remember that once you have started on the note E, you have to go up according to the same pattern of tones and semitones. The first two notes have been given. Check on page 76 to see if you are correct.

Here is the melody of *The Ash Grove* again, but in the new key of E major. The C major version is underneath, so you can see how the transposition simply moves all the notes up three places and adds the necessary accidentals.

Little Bo-Peep has been put up four notes, into F major. This time one note of the scale needs to be changed: every B is a B flat.

Key signatures

Look at the two versions of *The Ash Grove* below. The music in the second version sounds exactly the same as the first, but instead of putting all the sharps in as they occur in the music (immediately before each note), it shows all the sharps you need to play in E major at the start of the piece. (Look back at your E major scale on page 35 for a reminder if you need to.)

If you look at the four sharps shown at the beginning of the second version of the tune, you can see that they have been positioned on the stave to show which notes they refer to. The F sharp where top line F would be, and so on. This means that F, C, G and D are all sharpened every time they occur in this piece.

This arrangement of sharps or flats at the beginning of a piece is called a key signature. It appears at the beginning of a piece and at the start of each new line of music. The sharp or flat signs shown mean that whenever you see that note, it will be a sharp or flat. This applies to any octave.

The key signature of C major has no sharps or flats

Here are some of the most commonly used key signatures:

G major with one sharp

D major with two sharps

A major with three sharps

F major with one flat

B flat major with two flats

E flat major with three flats

There are key signatures for every note of the chromatic scale. Learning all the key signatures takes time and generally musicians learn them gradually as they perform them. For the complete range of key signatures see pages 72-73.

Fast and slow

By now you should be able to read the pitch of a note and work out some of the rhythms that are made by combining the different types of notes and rests. Almost as important, when you are performing or reading a piece of music, is to know how fast (or slow) it should go. The speed of the beat is known as the tempo.

Metronome marks

The speed of the beat in a piece of music is usually given at the beginning. The tempo can be shown either by words or by a metronome mark. The metronome mark (sometimes abbreviated to MM) shows how many beats per minute there should be. Some musicians refer to this as b.p.m. Any metronome should have indications showing the speeds referred to, so that the tempo is quite easy to find.

> A metronome is an instrument used to set the speed of a piece of music. It can be set to click a certain number of beats per minute.
>
> ♩ = 60
>
> This metronome marking shows there are 60 beats per minute, or a beat every second

If the speed is indicated in words, it is very often given in Italian. This is because Italy was where music was first printed, and the terms have become standard for musicians in every country. Here are some of the most common Italian instructions.

Adagio means slowly.

Allegro means lively.

Andante means moderately slowly, or at a walking pace.

Largo or *Lento* means very slowly.

Moderato means moderately.

Presto means fast.

This is Handel's famous *Largo...*

Vivaldi's *Spring* from *The Four Seasons* starts allegro...

48

49

When two notes of the same pitch are joined by a slur, it is called a tie. Ties make two notes sound like one.

Putting it all together

Listen to the three tracks 50, 51 and 52 on your CD. The music to each is on the opposite page.

Some of the features in this music are marked by a letter. See if you can match each letter to the correct name below.

Dotted crotchet
(dotted quarter note) _ _ _ _ _ _ _ _

Flat sign _ _ _ _ _ _ _ _

Key signature _ _ _ _ _ _ _ _

Minim (half note) rest _ _ _ _ _ _ _ _

Piano (quiet)
indication _ _ _ _ _ _ _ _

Quaver (eighth note) rest _ _ _ _ _ _ _ _

Sharp sign _ _ _ _ _ _ _ _

Slur _ _ _ _ _ _ _ _

Staccato mark _ _ _ _ _ _ _ _

Tempo indication _ _ _ _ _ _ _ _

Now have a look at page 76 to check the answers.

Play the three melodies on the CD again, and listen carefully for the effect that all the indications you listed above have on the music. You may find it easier to follow each of these elements separately until you are familiar with the melody.

Remember to check:
• the tempo (speed)
• the articulation (legato, staccato and accents)
• the accidentals (sharps and flats)
• the rhythm (lengths of notes and rests)
Finally, don't forget to follow the pitches of the notes as they rise and fall to make the shape of the melody.

Follow the music below while you listen to track 53. Then try to write in all the elements which are on the CD but are missing from the written music.

Look out for dynamic markings (loud and soft), phrasemarks, staccato notes, accents, missing accidentals and so on!

Andante from Mozart's Serenade K203

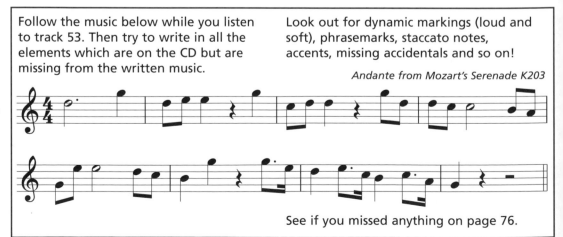

See if you missed anything on page 76.

from Mozart's String Quartet in D K499

from Schumann's Piano Concerto

from Brahms' Song of the Lord of Falkenstein

Minor scales

So far, almost all the melodies we have looked at have been in major keys – that is, based around the notes of major scales. Listen again to track 4 for a reminder of how a major scale sounds. Now listen to the scale of C minor on track 54. Can you hear the difference between the two scales? Many people think that minor scales sound sad – this may be because they have a different arrangement of tones and semitones.

How the minor scale is made

There are several different types of minor scale, but they all have one thing in common – instead of starting **TONE TONE SEMITONE** like major scales, they begin **TONE SEMITONE TONE**. After that, the tones and semitones are arranged differently depending on the type. You can find out more about this on the following page.

This diagram shows the notes of the C minor scale as they appear on a keyboard. Listen to the minor scale (track 54) again and try to follow the intervals.

Look at the scale of E minor (opposite), then Schubert's song *Aufenthalt* below. Listen to this minor melody on track 55.

How major and minor scales are related

For each major scale, there is minor scale with the same key signature. This is called the relative minor. If you look at the key signature of *Aufenthalt* you'll see that it has the same key signature as G major: one sharp. This is because it is in G major's relative minor key: E minor. Every minor scale has the same key signature as the major scale three semitones above it.

Here is how E minor is written with a key signature. It is exactly the same as the key signature for G major, but the scale begins on E instead and goes up TONE SEMITONE TONE.

More about minor scales

This next scale is the minor scale of B. If you count up three semitones from B you arrive at D, so D is the relative major. So B minor has the same two sharps in the key signature (F and C).

Can you write out a scale of D minor in the space provided?
* First write down the notes from D to D (the first note has been given).
* Next, work out the relative major by counting up three semitones and write in the key signature.

Check on page 76 to see how you did!

Different types of minor scale

The type of minor scale we have been looking at so far is called the natural minor. Two other sorts of minor scale are the harmonic and the melodic minors.

The key signatures of minor scales, whatever type they are, are the same as their relative majors. However, sometimes you need additional accidentals.

Harmonic minors

All harmonic minor scales contain a sharpened seventh note, but this accidental is not included in the key signature. It gives a distinctive tone-and-a-half interval (a tone plus a semitone) at the top of the scale. See if you can hear this interval in the scale of E harmonic minor on track 56.

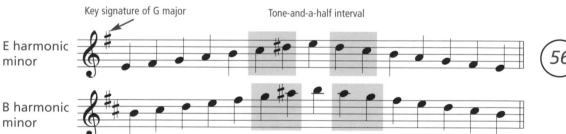

Melodic minors

This minor scale avoids the tone-and-a-half interval by raising the 6th and 7th notes on the way up and flattening them on the way down. Listen to E melodic minor on track 57 and see if you can hear the difference from E harmonic minor.

To see the full range of minor scales, see page 73

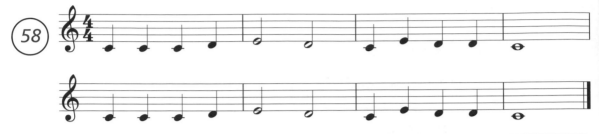

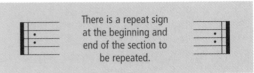

Repeats in music

Take a look at *Au clair de lune* below. Can you see that the melody consists of a four bar phrase which is repeated?

58

There is a sign in music which we can use to show that a section of music is to be repeated. The next example shows how *Au clair de lune* can be written using a repeat sign.

There is a repeat sign at the beginning and end of the section to be repeated.

If the repeat goes back to the start then the first repeat sign is not needed

The dots before the double bar-line are called a repeat sign. They tell you to play the music again.

There are many pieces of music which involve repeated sections, but with a slight change at the end. In the following song from *The Beggar's Opera,* the ending of the repeated section is slightly different. This means that we can't simply put repeat marks at the end of the first line. Instead we need a first-time bar and a second-time bar. The first time you'll hear the first-time bar. Then it will repeat from the first repeat sign. The second time you hear this section, the first-time bar is missed out and you'll hear the second-time bar.

Listen to the music on track 59, and see if you can follow the music through the first- and second-time bars.

59

You'll hear this bar the first time through...   ...and this bar the second time.

1.   **2.**

Different types of repeat signs

As well as the normal repeat marks, some pieces of music use signs and instructions which enable us to repeat certain parts of the music and to stop in different places. These instructions are often used in longer pieces, but for now let's see how the signs would work in *My Grandfather's Clock*.

As with tempo, repeat instructions are usually written in Italian. You will have to learn what they mean to follow a piece of music.

Da Capo (or D.C.) is Italian for 'from the head', or in other words, from the beginning. Used on its own, this instruction simply means that the whole piece is to be repeated.

Da Capo (or D.C.) al fine is more usual. 'Fine' is Italian for 'the end', so this instruction tells us that we should repeat the piece from the beginning, but then stop when we come to the 'fine' sign.

In the next version of *My Grandfather's Clock*, the first section does not repeat exactly. This time extra notes have been added (bars 4 to 8). If we just want to repeat this section at the end, we need a new instruction!

Dal Segno (or D.S. or D.%) al fine is Italian for 'from the sign to the end' and it tells us to repeat back to wherever the 'segno' (%) appears, and carry on until you reach the 'fine' sign.

Intervals

An 'interval' is the distance between any two notes. Different intervals give a melody its shape.

Major 3rd

(1   2   3)

When working out an interval, always count both the lower and upper notes. So for example, C to E is counted as a 3rd, and C to A is a 6th.

Major 6th

(1 2 3 4 5 6)

These are called major intervals because the notes occur in the major scale.

minor 6th

Look at the C minor scale opposite. If you count up three notes in this scale you come to E flat instead of E, which gives you an interval of a minor 3rd. The same is true of the interval of a 6th: if you come to A flat instead of A, the interval is a minor 6th.

minor 3rd

(60) Compare the major third and sixth with the minor third and sixth on track 60.

How many semitones?

If you look at the notes on the keyboards below, you can see that a minor third is an interval of 3 semitones and the major third is made up of 4 semitones.

In the same way, the minor 6th is an interval of 8 semitones and the major 6th one of 9 semitones.

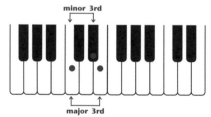

minor 3rd

major 3rd

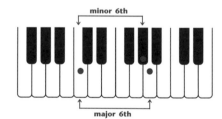

minor 6th

major 6th

More intervals

In fact, there is a name for every interval, from the interval of one semitone right up to an octave. You can see all of these on the next page. Although we are showing all the intervals from the note C, an interval can of course be from any note.

Each degree of the scale is included. Any interval rising from say C to F will be a fourth of some kind (either perfect or augmented). Any interval rising from C to B will be a seventh (either major or minor).

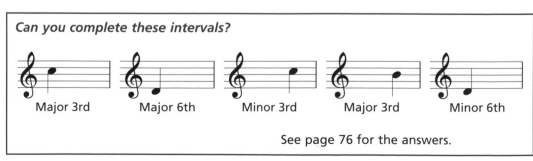

Can you complete these intervals?

Major 3rd   Major 6th   Minor 3rd   Major 3rd   Minor 6th

See page 76 for the answers.

The complete range of intervals

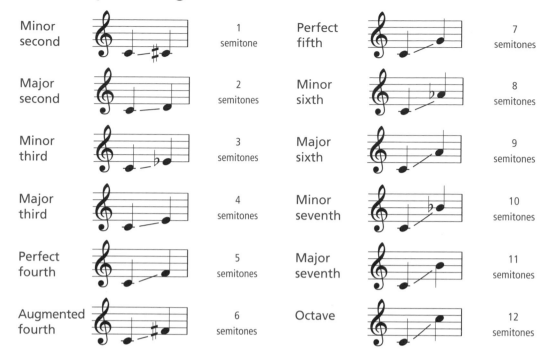

Minor second	1 semitone	
Major second	2 semitones	
Minor third	3 semitones	
Major third	4 semitones	
Perfect fourth	5 semitones	
Augmented fourth	6 semitones	
Perfect fifth	7 semitones	
Minor sixth	8 semitones	
Major sixth	9 semitones	
Minor seventh	10 semitones	
Major seventh	11 semitones	
Octave	12 semitones	

All intervals have the same number of semitones whatever note they start from. So with practice you should be able to recognise each interval and hear in your head how it will sound. If you can do this with any interval, no matter what the notes, you will be able to read any line of music and imagine how it will sound!

This does take a great deal of practice, but many people find it helps to remind them by thinking of intervals in well-known songs. Some examples are given below which may help you. Try to write down any others you can think of after these examples.

While shep - herds watched their flocks

Twin - kle, twin - kle

A - way in a ___ man - ger

Can you name these intervals?

-------------- -------------- -------------- -------------- -------------- --------------

See page 76 for the answers.

A new time signature

So far, most of the pieces have been in 2, 3 or 4 crotchet (quarter note) beats in a bar. There are other time signatures which count in different beats, however.

Compound time

Listen to track 61 and tap along with the beat of the music. Two beats are given before the music begins and the beats for the first two bars are also given. Now look at the music for this example. The beats for the first two bars are marked.

Can you see that each beat contains three quavers (eighth notes)? This is the first melody we have seen with the beats divided into three rather than two. This type of rhythm is known as 'compound time'.

beats: 1   2   1   2

6/8 time signature

You may already have noticed the new time signature. 6/8 means that there are six quavers (eighth notes) in each bar.

Listen to *Silent Night* again. It is a good example of the 'rocking' feeling which is typical of the 6/8 key signature. Can you tell what key it is in? (The answer is on page 76.)

The top number tells you there are six quavers in each bar (two beats of 3 quavers)

The 8 on the bottom means quavers or eighth notes.

More time signatures

A compound time signature can have more than two main beats to the bar. As each beat divides into three, the top number must be 6 (for 2 main beats), 9 (for three main beats) or 12 (for 4 main beats). It is very unusual to have a compound time signature with more than 12 beats in the bar.

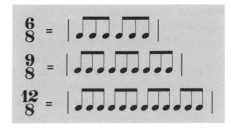

Here are melodies in 9/8 and 12/8:

A piece of music can have any number of beats per bar. A number of pieces use 'odd' five and seven beat rhythms. Two of the best known five-beat pieces are the first movement of Holst's *The Planets* and the second movement of Tchaikovsky's *Pathétique Symphony*. Try to listen to both of these. Here is part of an English folk song in 5/4.

Lower numbers in time signatures

The lower number in a time signature can also alter. We've already seen that it can be 4 (if the beats are crotchets) or 8 (for compound times, with dotted crotchet beats). But lower numbers can also be 1 (semibreve beats), 2 (minim beats), or 16, 32, or 64 for shorter notes. Of these, 2 (minim beats) is the most common. Here are some minim-beat time signatures.

Reading music with words

If the music you are reading is a song, then you will need to know how words and music are written to fit together.

Here is the beginning of the folk song *The Ship in Distress*, which was our example of 5/4 time. This time the words are given too. Listen to it again and see if you can sing along with the melody.

Usually there is one music note for each syllable of a word, so the two-syllable word 'seamen' has two notes, and is divided with a hyphen ('sea-men') to show which part of the word goes with each note.

The word 'landsmen' is also divided by a hyphen but is sung to four notes. The placing of the words under the notes clearly shows which notes to sing with each syllable. Try singing it, then listen to track 61 to see how you got on.

Setting many notes to one word

Sometimes, a composer writes a word to be sung to a long line of notes. The music below is *My Song Shall Be of Mercy and Judgement* by James Kent. He emphasises the word 'praises' by stretching the first

syllable over no fewer than 38 notes! When this happens, and the notes stretch beyond the end of the printed syllable, the word is continued with a line.

Putting it all together

Here are two musical examples with a few questions for you to answer. You can check your answers on page 77.

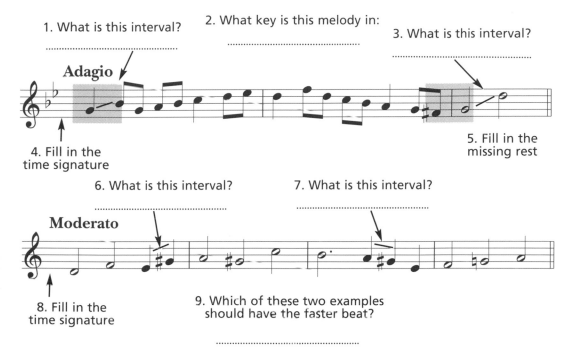

1. What is this interval?
2. What key is this melody in:
3. What is this interval?
4. Fill in the time signature
5. Fill in the missing rest
6. What is this interval?
7. What is this interval?
8. Fill in the time signature
9. Which of these two examples should have the faster beat?

Now look at the music below. Can you imagine how the piece will sound? Before you listen to the music try to 'hear' the tune in your head. Which bars repeat, and where does the piece end? Check track 63 see how close you were.

Scales

So far we've looked at three types of scale: chromatic (which has all twelve notes of the octave), and major and minor scales. These are not the only scales in music, however, and in this section we will look at some of the others.

The blues scale

This scale is very widely used, not only in blues, but in most popular musical styles.

A blues scale is made up of the 1st, 3rd, 4th, 5th and 7th notes of a major scale, then flattening the third and the seventh. If we try this in C major we get a blues scale in C. The F sharp (an augmented fourth) has been included although it isn't strictly part of the blues scale, because it is a common feature in blues music. Listen to the blues style 'riffs' on track 64. Can you tell what order the notes come in? (See page 77 for the answer.)

(64)

Can you write out a blues scale in A on the staff below? Remember that when you flatten a sharp note, it becomes a natural (so it will need no accidental sign). Include the augmented fourth in your blues scale. You can check your answer on page 77.

The pentatonic scale

(65)

The pentatonic scale is found in European folk melodies, and it very often gives an 'oriental' sound. Track 65 is made entirely from the notes of a pentatonic scale.

The easiest example of a pentatonic scale is the black notes of a piano or keyboard. If we write these down, the scale looks like this:

As with all scales a pentatonic scale can start on any note. To be able to write and recognise this scale on any note, however, you need to know the pattern of intervals in a pentatonic scale:

TONE	TONE-AND-A-HALF	TONE	TONE	TONE-AND-A-HALF

Try writing a pentatonic scale starting on E flat. Check your answer on page 77.

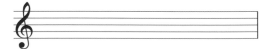

The whole-tone scale

This scale only uses intervals of a tone. Here is a whole-tone scale starting on C. If we start the scale a semitone higher it looks like the second example. In fact, there are only two versions of the whole tone scale. Whatever note you start on, it will give the same notes as one of these two examples.

The atmospheric music on track 66 uses the notes of the two whole-tone scales.

(66)

Can you tell when it changes from one whole-tone scale to the other?

New note divisions

We have seen how a crotchet is divided into two quavers, but what if we want to divide it into three? Listen to track 67. Three crotchet beats are given before the music starts, to give you the tempo.

Can you hear where the beat is divided into three? Look at the start of the music below as you listen again. The beats which are divided into three are indicated by a figure 3. These sets of three notes are called triplets.

Any note value which is usually divided in two can be split into three using a triplet. The triplet is written using note values half as long as the main note. So if we want to write a triplet which lasts for a minim, it is written using crotchets.

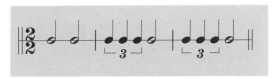

In fact, we can use this method to divide a single beat into any number we like. All we have to do is join up the group of notes with either the beam or with a bracket, then write the number of notes above or below it. Look at this melody taken from Chopin's *G Minor Nocturne*.

The beat highlighted has been divided into six, making a 'sextuplet'. These notes are written as semiquavers because the beat is divided into more than four.

In Chopin's B minor piano sonata (below), as well as the triplets there is a group of notes divided into five. This time the notes cover two beats. The pulse for this extract is given at the start of track 68. Can you feel how the five notes fit evenly into two beats?

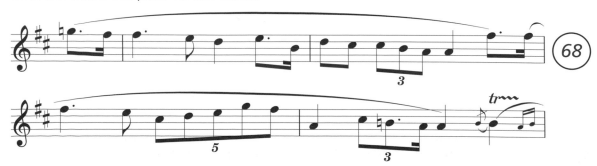

Simple chords

Like words, musical notes are read from left to right, and the notes appear in the order that we hear them. So it follows that if two notes appear above one another, they will be heard at the same time.

Any two notes which are vertically aligned are played together. When two or more notes sound together, this is known as a chord.

Below are two chords in the bass clef. The notes have been written out one at a time and then combined as a chord. Listen to track 69 to hear how the chords are built up.

Here is an extract from the slow movement of Mozart's piano concerto in C. If you just look at the lower staff, you will see the two chords from track 69. The first chord (F, A, C) is played for the first

three bars. It is in a triplet rhythm, so the chord plays three times for each of the four crotchet beats. In bars 4, 5 and 6 it changes to the second chord (E, B flat, C).

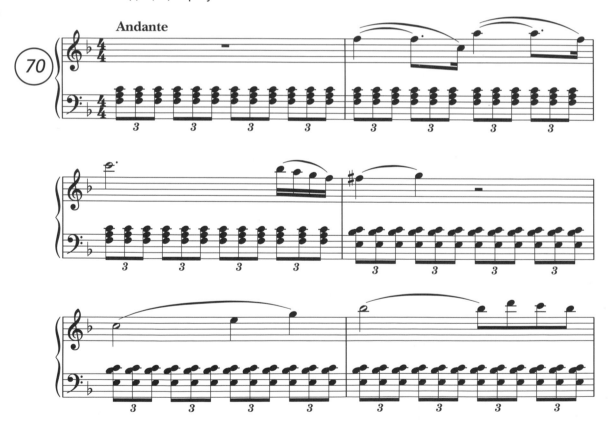

Now listen to this music on track 70. Try to hear where the chord changes come without looking at the music.

Musical form

On page 43 we saw how a melody could be extended using repeat marks or the indications 'Da Capo' or 'Dal Segno'.

Most pieces of music that you'll hear are more extended than this. They are made up of different sections arranged in certain patterns, such as the alternating verse/chorus pattern of a song.

Different sections in music can be identified by letters of the alphabet, which show clearly how the form is constructed. When a section is repeated with some modifications, the letter is followed a number 1.

Try to listen to the examples of each form given below, and see if you can identify the different sections.

Binary form

This is one of the simplest forms and consists of a piece of music in two sections.

The first section often modulates to the dominant (the key a fifth above). So if a piece begins in C major it would end the first section (A) on the dominant, G. The second section (B) then brings us back to the tonic (home key), using the same musical material.

Tonic to dominant | back to tonic

A / A1

Example: Prelude No. 20 in A minor from Bach's *48 Preludes and Fugues*, Book 2.

Ternary form

This consists of three sections. The second section usually forms a contrast to the first, often quieter and more lyrical. The first section then returns, generally with some changes.

This form is often used for the slow movement in classical symphonies.

Contrasting section

A / B / A1

Example: Slow movement from Dvořák's *New World Symphony*.

Variations

The most obvious way of extending a piece of music is by using variations. Music can be altered in many different ways: extra notes added, the harmonies (chords) altered, it can change from major to minor, and so on.

This can be an extremely effective form, far more interesting than it would at first appear!

A / A1 / A2 / A3 / A4 / etc.

Example: Mozart's piano sonata in A (K.331), first movement.

Minuet and trio

This is another form which is associated with symphonic movements, forming a contrast to the slow movement.

Overall it is a ternary form, with the minuet (a dance in 3 time) first, then the contrasting trio section (which is often written in three parts, hence its name), followed by a repeat of the minuet.

However, both the minuet and trio have two sections, (minuet A/B and trio C/D). The first time the minuet and trio are played, each section is repeated, but when the minuet returns at the end, the two sections are played unrepeated. So, altogether, the form looks like this:

A/A/B/B	C/C/D/D	A/B
Minuet /	**Trio** /	**Minuet**

Example: Mozart's piano sonata in A (K.331), third movment.

Rondo

Another popular form in classical music is the Rondo, often used for the last movement of a symphony.

Basically, the main A sction (usually a lively and energetic idea) alternates with other, contrasting sections. In fact, the pattern usually repeats one or two of the other sections as well, so that typical Rondo might look like the second example opposite.

A / B / A / C / A / D / A

A / B / A / C / A / B / A

Example: Mozart's piano sonata in A (K.331), last movement.

Sonata form

This is probably the most important form in all classical music. It can be found in virtually all sonatas, concertos and symphonies from before Mozart's time right up to the late Romantic period.
  The form is not always constant, and composers often make quite large changes to the pattern. Here is the basic structure, made up of three sections.

1. Exposition: the first section begins with a main melody (A) in the home key (tonic), which modulates to the dominant. A second, contrasting theme (B) appears in the new key.
2. Development: this section uses all the previous music, 'developing' it by altering aspects of it and changing the key.

3. Recapitulation: finally, the first section returns. This time, however, all the themes are in the home key.
There is often an extended ending, known as the Coda.

1. Exposition
Tonic to dominant   Remains in dominant
A / B

2. Development
Previous ideas developed
A + B

3. Recapitulation
Remains in tonic
A / B

Coda

Modern musical forms

The forms we have looked at so far, although still used today, refer more to classical than popular music. Pop songs tend to be based around a constant set of elements. Firstly there is an introduction, followed by a pattern of verses and chorus. There is then a 'middle 8' (so called because it is usually 8 bars long). Then either the verse or chorus repeats, and finally the song ends with a coda.

Introduction	Verse/Verse/Chorus B / B / C	Middle 8 D	Chorus C	Coda

As there is a lot of repetition in this form, rather than write it all out, a typical pop song uses repeat signs and *dal segno*. Rather than include a whole song, here is *Grandfather's Clock* arranged as a pop song in miniature. See if you can work out the repeats in the music before listening to it on track 71.

It is complicated, but a song would normally be easier to follow with words. However, it is very useful to be able to work out the geography of a song for yourself – otherwise you can get very lost trying to follow the music!

Reading different types of music

Voice and organ

This example for voice and organ is from *My Song Shall be of Mercy and Judgement* by James Kent. Each line of the score is made up of three staffs of music all joined together on the left of each line. Each of these lines is called a system. The bottom 2 staffs are bracketed together because they are both for organ (the upper part for right hand and the lower for left hand).

Most church organs have two or more 'manuals' (keyboards) which can be set to play different sounds. In line 2, 'Tpt.' is short for trumpet, and this part should be played on a manual set to a trumpet sound. At 'Sw.', which stands for swell (the upper manual) the organist returns to the normal accompanying sound. These changes mean that the organ can play in the background (on the swell) or play the melody as a solo or duet with the voice (trumpet).

String quartet

In this string quartet by Mozart there are four staves joined together, showing that four instruments play together. At the beginning of the piece, each line gives the name of the instument which plays it: *violino I, violino II, viola* and *violoncello*. All string quartets are written for this grouping of instruments. As in this score, instrument names are often given in Italian.

You can see by the shape of the musical lines that the four instruments play the same theme at the beginning, then some continue and some have a long held note. At bar 13, the instruments enter one at a time with a similar musical idea. This musical feature is known as imitation.

On scores like this you will usually find bar numbers and rehearsal figures. These are given in boxes and are either letters or numbers. They occur regularly throughout the score, and are useful for rehearsing or to refer to when analysing the music.

58

Orchestral score

This page from Tchaikowsky's *Romeo and Juliet* Overture has no fewer than 17 staves as well as 2 percussion parts written on single lines. This is the size of the orchestra in the late Romantic Period. The instrumentation of an orchestral score can vary a lot, but most of the standard orchestral instruments are here.

A modern score might have more percussion and some unusual instruments such as alto flutes or saxophones. The names of all the instruments here are given in Italian.

Often, as in this score, each woodwind part has two instruments playing. If you look at the two flutes in bar 150, you can see that there are two notes, so there must be two players. Can you work out what these very high notes are? (Answer on page 77.)

Orchestral scores always have woodwind instruments at the top, brass underneath, and percussion in the middle. Any keyboard instruments or harps are with the strings at the bottom. The violins are divided into two parts.

When you're reading an orchestral score, it is usually best to start by following the 1st violin part, as it has most of the melodic material and plays a lot of the time. Once you are used to this, you can start to look out for other instruments which have important passages to play.

Vocal score

If you sing in a choir, you may have to read from a vocal score, sometimes known as a short score. Here is the beginning of Handel's famous 'Hallelujah Chorus' from the *Messiah* as it appears in a vocal score.

In this example, the voices all move in the same rhythm, producing a series of chords.

In this piece the choir is divided into sopranos, altos, tenors and basses (often abbreviated to S.A.T.B.). Each voice has its own part to read.

The orchestral parts have been arranged so that they can be played on the piano. As well as saving space, this means the choir can practise without the orchestra.

Modern scores

This page from *Adiemus* by Karl Jenkins is an example of the kind of score often found in popular music or jazz. It is sometimes known as a 'fakesheet' because the player or arranger can adapt it to their own chosen style, using the chord symbols to create the harmony.

The chord symbols are printed above the music. The capital letter indicates the chord, which is made up of the 1st 3rd and 5th notes of the scale. For example, C tells you to play a C chord.

If the chord letter is followed by an **m**, then it is a minor chord. This is made the same way as a major chord, but uses the minor scale (so has a flattened third). The numbers refer to other degrees of the scale which can be added to the chord. There is a complete guide to chord symbols on page 74.

There is a simple version of the extract on track 72. Can you 'feel' the chord changes as they happen?

Transposing instruments

Look again at the Tchaikowsky score on page 58. Did you notice that not all of the instruments have a key signature of two sharps? The clarinet, for instance has one flat in the key signature.

This is because they are transposing instruments. This means that the note that is written for them is not the same as the note which is heard. The reason for this goes back to the time before valves and keys, when a trumpeter, for instance, would need several different trumpets, each for playing in a different key (harmonica players still have to do this!). The result is that if a clarinet player plays a C, we hear a B flat. This means the music has to be written one note higher than normal, for us to hear the right note.

If you find this confusing, the best way to remember it is that a clarinet in B flat *sounds one note lower* than normal pitch (because B flat is one tone lower than C). A french horn in F sounds five notes lower than normal (because F is five notes lower than C), and so on.

Here are the transposing instruments you are most likely to come across. In each case, this is what you would have to write to get the first 5 notes of a C major scale.

Cor anglais and French horn (in F)
To hear:

(sounds a fifth lower than written)
you write:

Clarinet and Trumpet (in B flat)
To hear:

(sounds a tone lower than written)
you write:

Alto saxophone (in E flat)
To hear:

(sounds a major sixth lower than written)
you write:

Tenor saxophone (in B flat)

To hear:

(sounds an octave and a tone lower than written)
you write:

Ornaments

An ornament is a symbol used to indicate that extra notes can be added to the musical line, in order to decorate it.

Trills

The most commonly used ornament is probably the trill. This sign tells the performer to alternate rapidly between the written note and the one above it. Here is a short passage from Beethoven's piano sonata No. 28. On track 73 it is first played without the trill markings, then

with them added. You can imagine the amount of copying saved by using this simple sign!

Mordent

Sometimes the composer wants a simpler decoration. The mordent tells the performer to play the written note, then the one above, then the note again. Throughout the music below, Schubert adds mordents and grace notes to vary this melody, which occurs many times during the piece.

Lower mordent

The lower mordent is very similar, it simply moves to the note below rather than the one above. Here is an example from Bach's *Toccata, Adagio and Fugue in C.*

Adagio

Turn

The turn is like a mordent immediately followed by a lower mordent, decorating both above and below the main note. Sometimes the main note is sounded first, depending whether the symbol is positioned above or after the note.

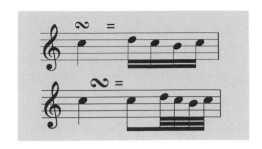

Here is an example, again from Beethoven's *Piano Sonata* No. 28.

Grace notes

Lastly, here is an example of grace notes. They are written very small and decorate a musical passage. These note values do not count as part of the bar, so the performer has to fit them in gracefully, taking a little time from one of the other notes.

Here is an example of music containing grace notes, from a Schubert *Impromptu*.

These are only some of the most common ornaments. Players who study baroque music, for example, must deal with many others, and study exactly how they fit with the music round them.

Musical shorthand

There are two types of musical shorthand which are very common in handwritten scores. They're both useful in music which has repeating patterns. Look again at the extract from Mozart's piano concerto in C on page 52. If you were copying it out by hand, you might write it like this:

If you compare the two versions, you'll see that whenever a pattern is repeated, you can write the symbol ⅞. to indicate this.

You can write the symbol across a whole bar to show that the previous bar is repeated (as we have done in bar 2) or you can write it across a single beat, to show that the music of the previous beat repeats.

Below is part of the score of Mozart's piano concerto in C. If you look carefully at the 2nd violin and viola parts you'll see notes with a line through the stem. They indicate that written note should be played as repeated quavers (or, in this case, quaver triplets, continuing the pattern established in the first bar). We know quavers are needed because the note is crossed by a single line (like the single tail on a quaver). If semiquavers were needed, then the stem would have two lines through it.

Here is another shorthand pattern which helps with pairs of repeating notes. The two notes to be played alternately (C and E in the example) are both written as minims, which is how long the pattern is played for. As you can see, the quaver pattern has a single tail and the semiquaver pattern has a double tail (just as with the single repeated note pattern). These are called tremolos.

More notes and rests

Now that you are familiar with most note lengths, it is useful to see a summary of them all and how they relate to each other. There are a few new ones too.

You may already have noticed that note lengths have two names. This is because the American names are different from the English.

Breves
This is the longest note of all. At one time, early in the history of musical notation, this was actually the shortest note, hence its name, the breve. It's probably easier to think of it as a double whole note.

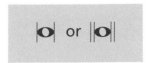

Demisemiquavers
Just as we added an extra line to a quaver to change it into a semiquaver, we can add another line to get a demisemiquaver, or 32nd note. This is half the length of a semiquaver, so there are eight of these to a single crotchet.

Hemidemisemiquavers
Hemidemisemiquavers or 64th notes are quite rare. Again the value is halved, so that there would be 16 of these to a single beat.

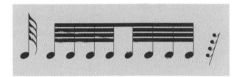

You could carry on adding lines to get a 128th note, and so on, but obviously these are hardly ever needed.

Here is a table of all the note lengths and their names (English followed by American), with the equivalent rests.

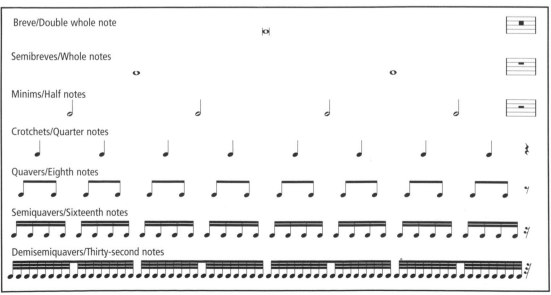

New names for old notes

Look at the keyboard diagram alongside. Which note is the arrow pointing at? It can either be called C♯ (as it is a semitone higher than C) or D♭ (as it is a semitone lower than D).

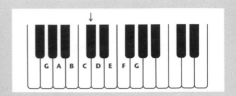

This is an enharmonic: using a different name for the same note.

Every note has an enharmonic alternative name.

The musical example below begins in E major. The second bar starts on G♯, and the third bar on A♭. This is exactly the same note as G♯ so is is known as an enharmonic change.

The music is actually modulating (changing key) from E major, which has four sharps, to A♭ major, which has four flats.

Here are the scales of E and A flat, written without key signatures. The notes they have in common are highlighted. All of these notes are notated differently in each key. This means that when we want to

modulate from E to A flat major, at some point we have to change from writing them as sharps to writing them as flats. In the melody above, this happens in the third bar.

In Schubert's song *On the Danube,* a similar enharmonic change happens, this time moving from a flat key to a sharp key. In bar 4, the same note appears twice,

first as a G♭ and then as an F♯.

Listen to the extract on track 74. Can you feel where the change of key happens?

Putting it all together

Here are extracts from four different types of music. There are various questions to answer as you listen to each one (the answers are on page 77), but the main thing is to enjoy following the different musical lines!

This impressive piano solo is from *Hungarian Rhapsody* by the great pianist Franz Liszt.

75

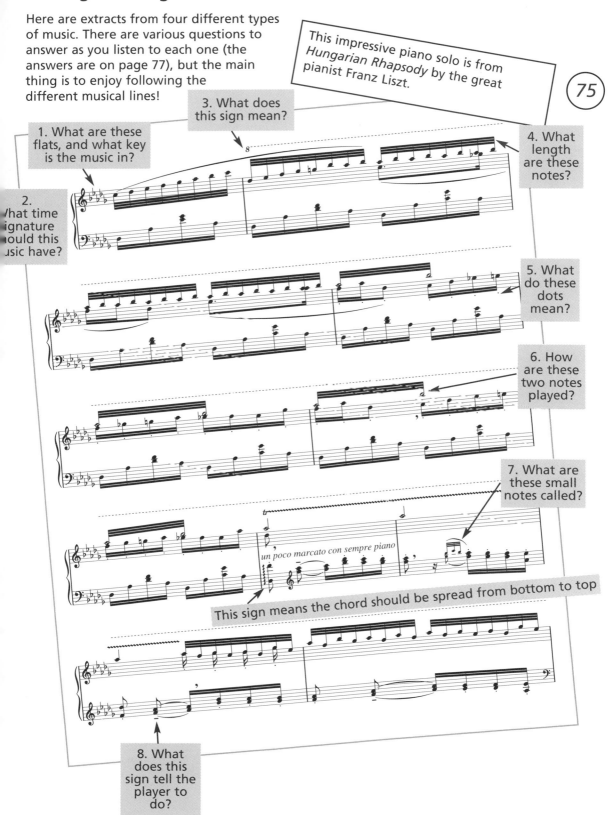

1. What are these flats, and what key is the music in?

2. What time signature should this music have?

3. What does this sign mean?

4. What length are these notes?

5. What do these dots mean?

6. How are these two notes played?

7. What are these small notes called?

This sign means the chord should be spread from bottom to top

8. What does this sign tell the player to do?

un poco marcato con sempre piano

This is from a *Sonata for cello and harpsichord* by J.S. Bach. There are three lines of music, one played by the cello, and the other two by the right and left hands on the harpsichord. The parts imitate and echo each other in a lively dance.

76

This sign stands for 2/2 time, also known as 'cut common' time.

1. What key is this sonata in?

Allegro moderato (♩ = 76-80)

(*mf*)   (*non legato*)

2. How long does this rest last?

3. What is this ornament?

4. What is this ornament?

5. What is this interval?

The instrument names are given here in German.

1. Can you tell from the CD which instrument is playing the melody?

This is the beginning of the slow movment of Brahms' *Violin Concerto.* The piece is for full orchestra and violin, but here, just the wind and horns are playing.

77

2. What does Adagio mean?

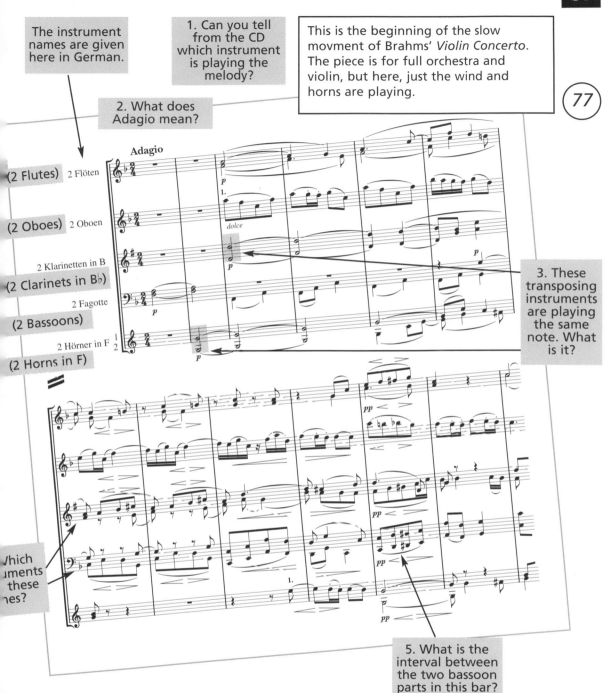

(2 Flutes) 2 Flöten

(2 Oboes) 2 Oboen

2 Klarinetten in B
(2 Clarinets in B♭)

2 Fagotte
(2 Bassoons)

2 Hörner in F ½
(2 Horns in F)

Adagio

dolce

3. These transposing instruments are playing the same note. What is it?

Which ...uments ... these ...nes?

5. What is the interval between the two bassoon parts in this bar?

Italian terms

Here are some of the more common Italian terms used in music.

a cappella   voices alone (without accompaniment)
accelerando   becoming faster
adagietto   slightly faster than *adagio*
adagio   slowly
adagissimo   extremely slowly
a due   played by two players
affetuoso   affectionately, tenderly
affrettando   hurrying
agitato   with agitation, excitedly
alla breve   in 2/2 time rather than 4/4
al coda   go to the *coda*
al fine   until the end or the *fine* mark
alla marcia   in the style of a march
alla misura   in strict time
allargando   slowing down, broadening
allegramente   in a lively way
allegretto   slightly less fast than *allegro*
allegro   lively
al segno   go to the sign
amabile, amoroso   lovingly
andante   moderately slowly (at a walking pace)
andantino   slightly faster than *andante*
animando/animato   becoming more animated
appassionato   with passion
appena   scarcely, barely
arco   using the bow [strings]
arioso   in the style of an operatic aria
assai   much or very much (e.g. *allegro assai*)
a tempo   back to the main speed
attacca   straight on, with no pause

basso/bassa   low
bellicoso/bellicose   martial or warlike
ben/bene   sufficiently, well
breve/breva   short (usually used for pauses)
brillante   brilliantly

calando   decreasing in both speed and volume (dying away)
calmato/calmando   more calmly
cantabile/cantando   with a singing quality
capriccioso   capriciously
chiaro   clearly
come prima   as at the beginning or 1st time
con amore   lovingly
con bellezza   beautifully

con bravura   with boldness
con brio   with spirit
con chiarezza   clearly
con espressione   expressively
con forza   with force
con fuoco   with fire
con grandezza   grandly
con grazia   with grace
con gusto   with gusto, enthusiasm
con moto   with motion/movement
con pedale   with (sustaining) pedal [piano]
con sordino (con sord.)   with the mute
con spirito   with spirit
con tenerezza   with tenderness
con tutta forza   as loudly as possible
crescendo (cresc.)   becoming gradually louder

da capo (D.C.)   repeat from the beginning
dal segno (D.S.)   repeat from the sign
deciso   decisively, resolutely
decrescendo (decresc.)   becoming gradually softer
delicato   delicately
diminuendo (dim.)   becoming quieter
divisi (div.)   divided (different notes played on separate instruments, rather than chords)
dolce   sweetly
dolente/doloroso   sadly

eguale   with an even tone
energico   energetically
espressivo (espress.)   expressively

forte (f)   loudly
fortissimo (ff)   extremely loudly
fine   the end
furioso   furiously
forzando (fz)   with sudden force (accented strongly)

giocoso   with humour
giusto   exact (as in *tempo giusto* – return to exact tempo)
glissando   slide from one pitch to another
grandioso   grandly
grave   very slowly – slower than *adagio*
grazioso   gracefully

lacrimoso   mournful, tearful
lamentoso   lamentingly
largamente   broadly
larghetto   slightly faster than *largo*

largo   very slow
legato   smoothly
leggiero   lightly
lentamente   slowly
lentissimo   extremely slowly
lento   slowly
liberamente   freely
l'istesso tempo   tempo stays the same

maestoso   grandly
marcato   stressed, emphasised
marziale   in a military manner, martial
meno   less
mesto   sadly, mournfully
mezzo forte (mf)   medium loud
mezzo piano (mp)   medium quiet
misterioso   mysteriously
moderato   at a moderate speed
molto/molta   much, very
morendo   dying away
mosso   agitated

nobile/nobilmente   nobly

obbligato   required, obligatory
ossia   alternatively (indicates an alternative version of a passage of music)

parlato   spoken (rather than sung)
passionato   with passion
patetico   with great emotion
pedale (ped.)   pedal
perdendosi   dying away
pesante   heavily
piacere, a   as the performer pleases,
piacevole   pleasantly, agreeably
piangendo   plaintively, as if crying
pianissimo (pp)   extremely quietly
piano (p)   quietly
più   more
pizzicato (pizz.)   plucked [strings]
placido   tranquilly
poco   a little (e.g. poco a poco – little by little, gradually)
precipitoso   precipitously, quickly
preciso   precisely
prestissimo   extremely fast
presto   very fast
prima volta   the first time

quasi   almost, as if
rallentando (rall.)   slow down
rinforzando (rinf, rfz)   suddenly stronger

risoluto   resolutely
ritmico   rhythmically
ritardando (rit.)   slowing down gradually
ritenuto   held back
rubato   in a free rhythm

scherzando   jokingly, wittily
secco   drily, short and detached
segue   carry on without a break
semplice   simply
sempre   still, always
senza   without
sforzando (sf, sfz)   a sudden forced accent
slentando   becoming slower
smorzando   dying away
soave   gently, sweetly
sonore   sonorously
sordino (sord.)   mute, damper
sospirando   as if sighing
sostenuto   sustained (often implying a slowing of the tempo)
sotto voce   sung in an undertone
staccatissimo   each note as short and detached as possible
staccato   each note short and detached
stesso   the same
strepitoso   noisily, boisterously
stringendo (string.)   pressing on, becoming faster
subito   suddenly

tacet   remain silent
tempo   speed, pulse
tempo primo   return to the original tempo
teneramente   tenderly
tenuto (ten.)   held, sustained
tranquillo   calmly
troppo   too (as in allegro ma non troppo – lively, but not too much)
tutta forza   as loudly as possible
tutti   all, a passage where all the musicians play, as opposed to just the soloist(s)

veloce   fast
vibrato (vib.)   a rapid small fluctuation in pitch
vigoroso   with vigour
vivace   in a lively manner
vivo   in a lively manner
voce   voice
volante   soaring, flying
volti subito (V.S.)   turn the page

Complete major and minor scales

	Key signature	Scale		Chord

C major

G major

D major

A major

E major

B major

Note:
F♯ major
is the
same as
G♭ major

F sharp major

G flat major

D flat major

A flat major

E flat major

B flat major

F major

Relative minors:

A minor

E minor

B minor

F sharp minor

C sharp minor

G sharp minor

D sharp minor

Note:
D♯ minor
is the
same as
E♭ minor

E flat minor

B flat minor

F minor

C minor

G minor

D minor

Chord symbols

C

When chord symbols are used (as on page 60) a single capital letter indicates a major chord. So C would mean C major, D would be D major and so on. To find the notes of a C chord, take the first, third and fifth notes of the major scale.

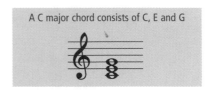

A C major chord consists of C, E and G

Cm

A small letter 'm' after the chord letter indicates that the chord is minor. To find the notes of a C minor chord take the third note of the major scale (the E) and flatten it (E flat).

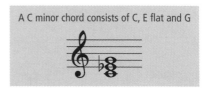

A C minor chord consists of C, E flat and G

C⁷

A small number 7 after the chord letter shows that the chord has the flattened seventh of the scale added to it. To find the notes of a C seventh chord take the seventh note of the major scale (the B) and flatten it (B flat). This is added to the normal major chord.

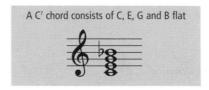

A C⁷ chord consists of C, E, G and B flat

Cᵈⁱᵐ

If the abbreviation 'dim' appears after the chord letter, it is a diminished chord. To find the notes of a C diminished chord take the normal major chord, then flatten the third (to E flat) and the fifth (to G flat), then add the sixth note of the scale.

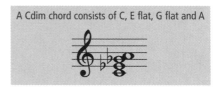

A Cdim chord consists of C, E flat, G flat and A

You can spot a diminished chord because it is made up of minor third intervals.

Answers

Page 14

(Haydn Surprise Symphony) ⑬

(Little Bo-Peep) ⑭

(Widdecombe Fair) ⑫

Page 18 the Gs are an octave apart.

(Eine Kleine Nachmusik)

Page 20

C D E F G A B C   C D E F G A B C

The scale covers two octaves.

Page 21
The music starts on middle C.
The notes are:
C C C D C C G A G A B C C

There are four beats in each bar.
The tune is *Good King Wenceslas.*

Page 27 In this piece, the rests help
punctuate the phrases.

(The Ash Grove)

Page 31

F♯   C♯   Add ♮ sign

Answers (contd.)

Page 35

Page 38

Dotted crotchet = b	Quaver (eighth note) rest = d
Flat sign = f	Sharp sign = g
Key signature = i	Slur = e
Minim (half note) rest = c	Staccato indication = h
Piano (quiet) indication = a	Tempo indication = k

Page 41

Page 44

Major 3rd   Major 6th   Minor 3rd   Major 3rd   Minor 6th

Page 45

Major 2nd   Octave   Perfect 4th   Minor 3rd   Minor 7th   Major 6th

Page 46

Silent Night is in D major.

Answers (contd.)

Page 49
1. Minor 3rd
2. G minor
3. Perfect 5th
4. 5/4
5. Crotchet rest
6. Major 3rd
7. Minor 2nd
8. 3/2 or 6/4
9. The 2nd example: although example 1 has shorter note values, it has a slower pulse (adagio is slower than moderato).

Page 50
Blues scale in A:

Pentatonic scale starting on E flat:

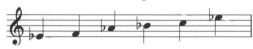

Page 58
The highest note is F, the lower note is C.

Page 67
1. The flats are B, E, A, D and G. The key is D flat major.
2. The time signature should be 2/4.
3. The notes are an octave higher than written.
4. Demisemiquavers (or 32nd notes).
5. Staccato dots mean the notes are short and detached.
6. The two notes are played as a tremolo.
7. Grace notes.
8. Play the note with an accent.

Page 68
1. The key is G major.
2. A minim rest lasts for 2 beats.
3. A trill.
4. A turn.
5. A minor 6th.

Page 69
1. The first oboe.
2. Slow.
3. Octave Cs.
4. The clarinets and bassoons.
5. An octave.

Reminders

Accent (28)
Accidental Symbols which make the pitch of a note sharper or flatter. (30)
Adagio Italian word for slow. (37)
Allegro Italian word meaning lively. (37)
Andante Italian word meaning moderately slowly, or at a walking pace. (37)
Articulation (28)

B minor scale (41)
Bar A unit of musical time. Bars are divided into *beats* and separated by barlines. (9)
Bass clef The *clef* used for low pitch notes. (19, 20)
Beat The regular pulse of a piece of music. (8)
Binary form (53)
Blues scale (50)
Breve (65)

C major scale (29)
C minor scale (40)
Chord Two or more notes sounded together. (52)
Chord symbols Letters which indicate the chord which should be played. (74)
Chromatic scale A scale which uses all the notes of the keyboard, black and white. (29)
Clef The sign at the beginning of a piece of music that tells you how high or low the notes are. (6)
Compound time (46, 47)
Crotchet (11)

Da capo (DC) A type of *repeat* that tells you to go back to the beginning of a piece. (43)
Dal segno (DS) A sign used to tell you to repeat a certain section of the music. (43)
Demisemiquaver (65)
Dotted notes (26)
Double whole note (65)
Dynamics (28)

E minor scale (40, 41)
Eighth note (22)

Fine Italian word for finish. (43)
First-time bar A type of *repeat*. (42)
Flat A symbol that lowers a note by a semitone. (30)

Form (53, 54, 55)
Four-beat note A four-beat note is called a semibreve or whole note. (10)
Grace notes (63)

Half-beat note A half-beat note is called a quaver or eighth note. (22)
Half note (11)
Harmonic minor (41)
Hemidemisemiquaver (65)

Interval The distance between any two notes. (44, 45)
Imitation (57)

Key A set of particular notes on which pieces and *scales* are based. (34)
Key signature A set of *sharps* or *flats* at the beginning of a piece. (36)

Largo Italian word for very slow. (37)
Legato Italian word for smoothly. (28)
Leger line A small line above or below the *staff*. Notes which are not on the lines or in the spaces of the staff are written on leger lines. (19)
Lower mordent (62)

Major scale A *scale* with a particular arrangement of *tones* and *semitones*. (29)
Melodic minor (41)
Metronome mark (37)
Minim (11)
Minor scale A scale with a particular arrangement of *tones* and *semitones*. (40)
Minuet and trio (54)
Moderato Italian word for moderately. (37)
Modern scores (60)
Mordent (62)

Natural A note that is neither *sharp* nor *flat*. (30)
Natural minor (40, 41)
Note A single sound in a tune, written on the lines or in the spaces of the staff. (6)

Octave The gap between one note and the note with the same name above or below it. (18)
One-beat note A one-beat note is called

a *crotchet* or *quarter note*. (10, 11)
Orchestral scores (58)
Organ music (56)
Ornament Symbol indicating that extra notes should be added to the music, in order to decorate it. (62)

Pentatonic scale (50)
Phrase-marks (27)
Pitch The height or depth of a note, in science measured in hertz. (6)
Presto Italian word meaning fast. (37)

Quarter-beat note A quarter-beat note is called a semiquaver or sixteenth note. (26)
Quarter note (11)
Quaver (22)

Relative minor (40)
Repeat sign A sign that tells you to play a section of the piece again. (42)
Rest A period of silence. Like notes, rests last for different lengths. Different rests are shown by different symbols. (15, 22, 26, 65)
Rhythm A pattern of long and short sounds in a piece of music. (8)
Rondo (54)

Scale A chain of notes in a particular order. (34, 40, 50)
Second-time bar A type of *repeat*. (42)
Semibreve (11)
Semitone The smallest distance between two notes. (29)
Sharp A symbol that raises a note by a *semitone*. (30)
Sixteenth note (26)
Sixty-fourth note (65)

Slur A sign linking notes together so they are played smoothly. (28)
Sonata form (54)
Staccato An Italian word meaning separated. A dot above or below a note tells you it is staccato – short and separated from the next note. (28)
Staff The set of five lines on which music is written (also called a stave). (6)
String quartet music (57)
System A line of music in a score (56)

Tempo The speed of the beat in a piece of music. (37)
Ternary form (53)
Thirty-second note (65)
Tie (37)
Time signature Two numbers, one above the other, which tell you how many *beats* are in a *bar*. The top number tells you how many beats to count, the bottom number tells you what type of beat. (13, 46, 47)
Tone The distance between a note on the keyboard and a note two keys (black or white) away from it. (29)
Transposition (35, 61)
Treble clef The *clef* used for high-pitch notes. (6)
Tremolos (64)
Trill (62)
Triplet A single beat divided into three. (51)
Turn (63)
Two-beat note A two-beat note is called a *minim* or *half-note*. (10, 11)

Variations (53)

Whole-tone scale (50)
Whole note (11)

For your notes